TRENT EDITIONS

Trent Editions aims to recover and republish landmark texts in handsome and accessible modern editions.

Editors: **Professors Sharon Ouditt** and **Andrew Thac**ker
Nottingham Trent University
Department of Arts and Humanities

Laura (Riding) Jackson Series / Series Editor:
Mark Jacobs

The Person I Am by **Laura (Riding) Jackson**, 2 vols.
edited by John Nolan and Carroll Ann Friedmann, 2011

Our other series are:

American Recoveries
Key texts from the cultural memory of North America

Early Modern Writing (silver covers)
Recovering radical manuscript & printed texts from the cultural margins

Poetry Recoveries
Reconnecting poets to their own time and ours
Postcolonial Writings (maroon covers)
Radical voices of the colonial past, speaking to the post colonial present

Radical Recoveries
The history & development of working-class, radical & popular print culture

For further information please contact Trent Editions, School of Arts and Humanities, Nottingham Trent University, Clifton Lane, Nottingham NG11 8NS, or use your internet search engine to find our web page.

POET: A LYING WORD
by
LAURA RIDING

A new edition
of the 1933 collection
edited and with an introduction
by
Jack Blackmore

Trent Editions
Nottingham Trent University

Poet A Lying Word, first published, London: Arthur Barker Ltd 1933
The First Leaf, first published Majorca: Seizin Press 1933
The Second Leaf, first published Majorca: Seizin Press 1935

This edition published by Trent Editions, 2017
Trent Editions
Department of Arts and Humanities
Nottingham Trent University
Nottingham NG11 8NS

Cover portrait of Laura Riding acquired by the Herbert F. Johnson Museum
of Art, Cornell University, through the generosity of the Sonia Raiziss Giop
Charitable Foundation. Photography courtesy of the Herbert F. Johnson
Museum of Art, Cornell University.

Design and typesetting by Trent Editions
Nottingham Trent University
Printed in Great Britain by ImprintDigital

ISBN 9781842331613

CONTENTS

PART III
Summer Never So Extreme, Nor Again

PART IV
Autumn's Last Word: Grief, Spite
And The Involuntary Smile Of Death

PART V
Failure Of Season

ADDENDUM

INTRODUCTION TO THIS EDITION

The blurb on the dustjacket of the original edition, no doubt the author's own, read:

> '*Poet: A Lying Word* is Laura Riding's first collected volume since *Poems: A Joking Word*, published over three years ago. In her previous work, Miss Riding has been bringing the language of poetic thought closer to its final energy and purity; and the influence of her work is apparent in the increasing precision with which contemporary poets express themselves. In this book one not only learns how to think poetically; one is in the country where poetry is the language spoken.'

1

The idea of reprinting this book emerged in the course of my study of Laura Riding's *Collected Poems*.[1] As I progressed through the poems of the author's 'self-determining canon' it became evident that the poems of her penultimate collection, *Poet: A Lying Word*, occupy a special place in the author's work, representing both a crisis in and the climax to her poetic career. The original edition of the book, published 84 years ago, is now rare. It has been seldom read, and less appreciated, even by the small band of those who admire her work. My own copy languished in the public libraries of Stepney and Croydon after 1934, apparently being issued only twice (presumably to the same reader) on 16 and 30 October 1976 before being withdrawn from circulation. Yet although Riding's poetry has been bypassed by the reading public, academic, critical or lay, she has been an acknowledged (and unacknowledged) influence on more than one generation of poets, including the far better known figures of Robert Graves, W.H. Auden, Ted Hughes, Sylvia Plath and John Ashbery.[2]

The poems of *Poet: A Lying Word* were all produced between 1930 and 1933, during the most settled period of Laura

Riding's poetic life. She had moved to Deià, Majorca with Robert Graves in October 1929 while recovering from her suicide attempt earlier that year. Then, in 1930, she published *Poems: A Joking Word* in which she effectively summed up her poetic career to that point. Meanwhile her new home and life were celebrated in one of her most accessible and attractive long poems, *Laura and Francisca*, published separately in 1931.

Poet: A Lying Word included nothing that had been published in *Poems: A Joking Word*, one indication of a break and a new direction after 1930 — about which there is much more to be said in the following section. *Poet: A Lying Word* is the most elaborately organised of her collections, divided into five parts, each with a mysterious rubric referring to the seasons, and their imminent demise, with the implication that we are heading 'out of time'. Part V is entitled 'Failure of Season', picking up on a theme from (amongst several other poems) the opening lines of the title poem:

> You have now come with me, I have now come with you,
> to the season that should be winter and is not: we have not
> come back.[3]

All fifteen poems in Part I were taken, some much altered, from the limited edition *Twenty Poems Less* (Paris: Hours Press, 1930) from which a further poem, 'Zero', was also chosen, rewritten and retitled 'The Flowering Urn' for Part IV. The twenty-one poems of *Twenty Poems Less* (ending, as in a countdown to blast-off, in 'Zero') often read like rough sketches for the more finished poems which appear in the subsequent volume.[4] Of the fifteen poems in Part II, the first seven — if the set of six fragments entitled 'Lines in Short Despite of Time' is counted as one — were extracted or adapted from another limited edition, *Though Gently* (Majorca: Seizin Press, 1930). The rest of the poems were new, with the exception of the long excerpts taken from *Laura and Francisca* which end Part IV.

Altogether, between the publication of *Poems: A Joking Word* in July 1930 and *Poet: A Lying Word* in December 1933 Riding had published four more volumes of poetry (the three mentioned above plus *The Life of the Dead* in 1933) and four other substantial prose works — a period of exceptional productivity.[5] Productivity of course is one thing, quality is another, and the rest of this introduction will argue that *Poet: A Lying Word* is the most original collection of poetry, and in important ways the finest, of the twentieth century.

2

What is the place of *Poet: A Lying Word* in the oeuvre of Riding? Joyce Wexler, the author of the first book about Riding, and the only one to attempt to describe her poetic development volume by published volume describes the work as a temporary aberration:

> For a brief period, Riding's pursuit of the essential led her to regret her need for language. By 1933, when she published *Poet: A Lying Word*, she expressed anger at the human need for words to articulate thought. Compared to perfect understanding of truth, human language seemed profane—a confining physical encumbrance. She mocked poets for pretending they had superior powers to perceive and reveal truth. The similarity of the title to her 1930 collection *Poems, A Joking Word* suggests that she intended to correct her earlier conception of the poet.[6]

The statements that she 'for a brief period' regretted the need for language, and that 'she expressed anger at the human need for words to articulate thought' are based, I think, on a misunderstanding of some poems, particularly 'Come, Words, Away'. By contrast with the eight pages devoted in her book to an account of just five of the poems of *Poet: A Lying Word*, Professor Wexler devotes twenty-two pages to ten of the later 'Poems Continual', praising and contrasting their serenity and 'impersonal perspective' with the 'wrestling' and the 'intensity of her personal involvement' (which is an accurate description, as we shall see, but need not be one of disparagement) in the preceding poems. As evidence that Riding herself did not view the volume as an aberration, she chose all but one of the poems in *Poet: A Lying Word* (the exception being 'Memory of the World') for her *Collected Poems* in 1938, and she subsequently chose nineteen of them, a higher proportion than from other volumes (or from 'Poems Continual') for her *Selected Poems: In Five Sets* in 1970.[7]

On the other hand Wexler, who deserves respect for her pioneering appreciation of Riding's poetry, was right to notice the differences between *Poet: A Lying Word* and the poetry that both preceded it and succeeded it. Riding herself, in one of her rare and valuable commentaries specifically upon her own poetry, remarked in 1972:

> Past the half-way mark, historically, in my poems, and up to the last phase, I am much preoccupied with the effort to make personally explicit the identity of myself poet and myself one moved to try to speak with voiced consciousness of the linguistic and human unities of speaking: I am restive insofar as this identity is only an implicit principle in my poetic speaking. There is also at work at the same time an effort to intensify in specificness the comprehensive reference I intended generally that my poems should have. The two heightened impulsions, working to bring within the poetic frame an explicitness and a specificness that it cannot contain and to which it cannot expand, produced within the poems themselves a struggle between compression and completeness of utterance. I cannot briefly make the explanation of the peculiarities of this phase[8] easier.

The half-way mark is clear in the sequence of her published poetry. Before the half-way mark are the poems of *Poems: A Joking Word* and after it come the poems collected in *Poet: A Lying Word*, which also preceded 'the last phase', represented by 'Poems Continual' in her *Collected Poems*. As noted above, all but one of the poems of *Poet: A Lying Word* were included in her *Collected Poems*: three ('Come, Words, Away', 'As to a Frontispiece' and 'Tale of Modernity') were placed towards the end of 'Poems of Immediate Occasion', the second of the four sections of the main body of *Collected Poems*, while the rest make up the entire third section, 'Poems of Final Occasion' — with the sole addition of the last poem there, 'Disclaimer of the Person'. There is no doubt that 'Disclaimer of the Person' belongs with the poems of *Poet: A Lying Word* as it exemplifies the 'heightened impulsions' described by the author above. It is an essential part of Riding's poetic apocalypse. For that reason, and also because the two parts of the first version of the poem, *The First Leaf* (1933) and *The Second Leaf* (1935) are very rare they are included as an addendum to this republication.[9]

The nature of the break, described so eloquently in the 1972 recording, between the earlier and the later work is in the nature of a life-changing category shift. My interpretation is that *Poet: A Lying Word* was the point at which she threw her all into the crucible of poetry to fulfil her spiritual — and at that time also her poetic — ambitions. This interpretation is in part supported by the blurb on the book's original dustjacket quoted in full at the beginning of this introduction: 'In this book one not only learns how to think poetically; one is in the country where poetry is the language spoken.'[10]

By contrast with the poems of *Poet: A Lying Word*, which are frequently (though by no means always) characterized by extravagant neologizing, riddling contradictions and paradoxes, and startling irruptions into the reader's consciousness, most of the 'Poems Continual' share, in line with Wexler's observations, a restrained elegance of phrasing, supple rhythms and a more conventionally 'poetic' beauty. This chimes with their author's retrospective commentary that 'A certain relaxing of the complex preoccupiedness I have described is perceptible in the very last phase.' It is as though this last period of poetic activity was to some extent a lap of honour, an exercise of her poetic gifts. At the same time she could explore the implications of her hard-won achievement in terms of: 'If what I've found out is true then how do I, how do you, live with that? How carry on from that foundation?' There is a sense that she had reached poetry's limit and was preparing to go beyond it. By 1935 she was already going further in prose (in some respects) than she could in poetry — in the ground-breaking essay 'The Idea of God', in *Epilogue*, for example, and in the writings on woman (and man) only gathered together for publication in *The Word "Woman"* after her death.[11]

This reference forward to the prose returns us to the place of *Poet: A Lying Word* in her poetry. As a reader progresses through the *Collected Poems* what had been implicit if not at all obvious in the earlier, more compact poems becomes overt in the more discursive poems taken from *Poet: A Lying Word*. There is a poem in which she meets and directly addresses 'God' ('Then Follows'); there are poems in which her cosmogony of 'sun' and 'moon' and 'earth' is unveiled ('Earth', 'All Things', 'Tale of Modernity' ['Bishop Modernity' in *PALW*], 'The Signs of Knowledge', Part I of 'Disclaimer of the Person' [*The First Leaf*]). She is ever more explicit about her understanding of what it means to be a woman, with examples throughout the collection, but notably 'Biography of a Myth', 'After Smiling' and 'The Dilemmist' ('Two Loves, One Madness' in *PALW*). She made direct reference to these features of her poems of this stage in her 1972 commentary:

> Two points of particular counsel may be useful. The first is generally applicable. Nowhere should I be taken as speaking by what are called 'symbols'. If, for instance I say 'the sun which multiplied' or 'the moon which singled' as I do in one poem, I am endeavouring to indicate actualities of physical circumstance in which our inner crucialities of human circumstance are set. My moon may look like the old tired poetical symbol, and I like an old tired poetic romanticist, but I truly meant that the moon's being what it is where it is intervenes in our outer circumstances as a negator of the sun's fostering excessiveness in our regard, both lush and destructive—as a tempering counter-agency, relatively little but near. However foolishly mystical this may seem, nothing so far learned by scientists or experienced by astronauts disproves this.

Before dismissing this disavowal of 'symbolism' out of hand it is worth considering how closely Riding's thought on poetic creativity and science compares with that of Coleridge. The latter had a belief in the unifying power of the 'esemplastic' (unifying, moulding into one) imagination, and developed 'Romantic epistemology', a theory of knowledge that went beyond the method of objective science. For him the driving force of the creative imagination to get at the inherent essence of external objects was love, a deep desire to know other than ourselves (the better to know ourselves). Compare Coleridge's 'esemplastic imagination' with Riding's reported view that she regarded a poet as 'dedicated very literally to the work of reconciling the separate things, the separate kinds of reality, into which existence is broken up—of finding the way in which they can be truly reconciled.' Neither Coleridge nor Riding was confined by professional boundaries to literature. Their thought, whether in poetry or prose, on matters of language or religion, was of a piece, connate.[12]

The paragraph quoted above continues:

> The second point of counsel concerns my use of the word 'woman' and the introduction of the fact of woman, in poems of this phase in particular. My use was literal on a large scale. I meant the common identity, woman, of women. I conceived of women under this identity as agency of the intrinsic unity-nature of being, and knew myself as of the personality of woman—as of this identity: and I endeavoured to make the poems include expressly the sense of this as it was actively present in me.[13]

To conclude this section then: *Poet: A Lying Word* functions in Riding's work as a book of revelation, or as she would put it in her 1938 preface 'an uncovering of truth', an uncovering of 'something that would otherwise remain unknown.'[14]

3

What kind of poet is Riding? Although she was, by the accident of her birth in January 1901 a 'century creature' and thus 'of this time', and she availed herself of the freedoms promised by the age, she does not fit at all comfortably into the category of 'modernist', for all that she (with Graves) had written with great sympathy for and understanding of modernist poets in *A Survey of Modernist Poetry* (1927).[15] In the 'Conclusion' of that work she had identified the new constriction caused by the critical self-consciousness that she found inhabited modernist poetry:

> As the poet, if a true poet, is one by nature and not by effort, he must be seen writing as unconsciously as regards time as his ordinary reader lives.

She saw critical self-consciousness as having had an inhibiting effect upon poets:

> The modernist poet therefore has an exaggerated preoccupation with criticism. [...] There is an increased strictness and experimenting in the construction of the poem, and an increased consciousness of what the poem should not be. But, so far, critical self-consciousness has been only a negative element in the making of poetry.[16]

These arguments at the conclusion of *A Survey* were Riding's and not Graves's. They were taken from Riding's *Contemporaries and Snobs*. This is the meaning of the note at the beginning of *A Survey* where the authors say:

> This book represents a word by word collaboration; except for the last chapter, which is a revision by both authors for the purposes of this volume of an essay separately written and printed by one of them.[17]

In *Contemporaries* Riding's argument as to the damage caused to poetry by the preoccupation with criticism (which is targeted primarily at the leading poet and critic of the day, T. S. Eliot), is developed even more trenchantly than in *A Survey*. (It is intriguing to recall that originally Graves had been planning to publish a work on modern poetry for Eliot's publishing house, Faber; the plan was superseded by the Riding-Graves collaboration.) The criticism of *poetry* in the previous chapters of *A Survey* becomes in its 'Conclusion' — and is even more so in *Contemporaries* — a criticism of *criticism* and of the institutional nature of literature itself:

> More and more the poet has been made to conform to literature instead of literature to the poet — literature being

the name given by criticism to works inspired by or obedient to criticism. Less and less is the poet permitted to rely on personal authority. The word *genius*, formerly used to denote the power to intensify a sense of life into a sense of literature, has been boycotted by criticism; not so much because it has become gross and meaningless through sentimentality as because professional literature develops a shame of the person, a snobbism against personal self-reliance which is the nature of genius. What is all current literary modernism but the will to extract the literary sense of the age from the Zeitgeist at any cost to creative independence?[18]

The arguments about 'increased strictness and experimenting in the construction of the poem' and critical self-consciousness as a negative element must also have been a description of her own experience as a poet in the modernist era. Her own poems display a great deal of both strictness and experimenting, and she herself, in the midst of her poetic career, devoted tremendous energy to criticism (although she was absolutely clear that poetry and not criticism had primacy). There is the strong sense in *Contemporaries* that she is wriggling free of the constrictions towards an assertion of her personal self-reliance and creative independence.

Then, in a series of essays in *Anarchism Is Not Enough* which was published only three months later Riding developed the positive obverse of the negative arguments of *Contemporaries* to set out her bold and sweeping vision for poetry and poets.[19] The comedy and sometimes the savagery of these essays have blinded readers to their seriousness, and to their direct relevance to an understanding of Riding's own poetry. In them is a defence of originality (in its deepest meaning) as the core value; of the person as the agent; and of poems as the process and product of the self's individuation. She is for analysis and opposed to synthesis; for 'impulsion' and opposed to reaction; she is for breaking down 'reality'; for the 'individual unreal' and against the 'social real'.

In some ways this language of genius and originality is familiar to us from the Romantics, but she (with Graves) had shown in *A Survey*, in a brilliant selection of almost indistinguishable passages from Shelley, Byron, Keats, Tupper, Wordsworth and Coleridge, how constrained these poets were (by contrast only with Blake) by 'spiritual elevation', by gentility and membership of the governing class: 'these poets only wrote authentic poetry when off their guard.'[20]

In the previous section I noted correspondences between Riding and Coleridge, although she (with Graves) brackets him with the other 'Romantic Revivalists' here. Riding's sympathies were clearly with Blake, and one can see the correspondences between them in the following passage:

> But he is a very rare instance of a poet who could afford not to affect a class-technique: for he was on intimate terms with the angels and wrote like an angel rather than like a gentleman. His radicalism was part of his religion and not a sentimentality as Wordsworth's early radicalism was. If a man has complete identity with his convictions, then he is tough about them, he is not sentimental; if not, then his convictions are a sentimental weakness however strongly he feels about them. The Romantic Revivalists were all spoiled as revolutionaries by their gentility. Blake was in no sense a Romantic Revivalist. He was a seer, or a poet. He despised the gentry in religion, literature and painting equally. That is why there is little or nothing of Blake's mature work that could be confused with that of any contemporary or previous writer.[21]

If the qualities she has in common with Coleridge are intellectual acuity and drive, and profound commitment to words, the qualities she shares with Blake are vision, identity with one's convictions, self-reliance and even genuine eccentricity. With both she shares a spiritual and religious quest that first finds expression in but is not confined to poetry. Going beyond literary correspondences there is something about Riding's career that reminds me of that of William Tyndale who paid with his life for his 'heresy' in translating the original Greek and Hebrew of the Bible into pithy, plain English, and demolishing the structure built by the established church on false premises based upon the Latin versions used hitherto. Riding of course lived on to a lively old age but could be said to have paid for her convictions with marginalization and misrepresentation.

Even before her 'renunciation of allegiance to [poetry] as a profession and faith in it as an institution' in her 1970 preface to her *Selected Poems,* her attacks upon its cherished traditions (of which more in section 6) amounted to poetic heresy, and would have offended and alienated literature's establishment and contemporary practitioners.

4

So much for the promissory advertisement. What about the poems themselves? Coming to them with an education in the tradition of poetry, they can seem so *peculiar* (to use her own double-edged word about her poetic originality in her manifesto poem 'As Well as Any Other'): they are so 'distinguished in nature or character', so 'unlike others, singular, unusual, odd' — that the reading mind struggles to grasp them.[22] They do not ingratiate themselves, or suggest that the poet is only saying what you have 'thought but ne'er so well expressed.' The poet's assumption of authority grates, for those used to a habitual self-deprecation in poets' presentation. The issue is acknowledged, with firmness and humour, in 'The Courtesies of Authorship':

> Now that you have read of,
> You will want to see.
> I can only take you to the place
> And let you not see.
> Then you may choose freely
> Between my book and your eye.
> You will undoubtedly prefer your eye,
> To not see for yourself.
> I shall be delighted to withdraw my book
> In favour of your however blind eye.
> But I will not withdraw my book

In favour of any book of yours,
In favour of time-begging prophecy.

There is too a lack of deference either to God or to nature; she had, as she says simply in 'Pride of Head', a very early poem, 'no precedent in nature.' As a poet she is *in action* on the universe in her poems, not *in reaction* to experience, which is what we are used to. And she does not leave us alone; she has (*pace* Keats) designs on us.

My suggestion is that it may be best in the first instance simply to read the poems in *Poet: A Lying Word*, or at least those that you can 'get into' straight through in one go. The remarkable range and scope of her poems should be evident at this first survey of the work — long poems and short, elegant and convoluted, gnomic and explicated, humorous as well as always grave. Each of the five parts builds up a momentum. In Part I it is fairly easy to grasp some of the meaning of the first two poems, 'As to a Frontispiece' and 'There are as Many Questions as Answers.' Each of these poems introduces language and themes which are developed throughout the book. Part I ends with the encounter with 'God' in 'Then Follows', when what follows is she herself writing poems ending in a sort of aspiration toward silence:

Ah, the pity of it for me,
To be by name a poet [. . .]
A creature neither man nor God. [. . .]

Ah the pity of it for you,
To be by nature man or by nature God,
And poet by name only to affirm
That beyond man and God lies only
Such beyond as poet alone can affirm,
Being creature of name only—
Ah the pity of it for us all.
Perhaps we had better not be going.
Perhaps I had better write another poem
And, if necessary, yet another,

Until a description follows
Of an interval after which
There's no return to time again,
To paradoxing truth between
Two similar poles of human logic—
After which no description
Unless words have wordless echo
As sound derived of silence
Might break unheard against itself
And echo silently
Through infinite parabolas
Of no description following.

Part II, which begins with poems from the highly experimental *Though Gently* is, in my experience, more difficult to enter, but 'The Biography of a Myth', 'The Wind, the Clock, the We' and 'The Talking World' are more accessible. 'The Biography of a Myth' makes a good introduction to the poet's story of woman and of herself, a story both mythical and yet intensely personal.

The pressure builds throughout Part II and is released in Part III into a powerful sequence of poems: 'After Smiling', 'It is not Sad', 'I Am' and 'As to Food', which develop further her story of woman and herself, and the relation between man and woman. It intensifies in an even more powerful sequence in Part IV: 'Bishop Modernity', 'Two Loves, One Madness', 'The Unthronged Oracle' and 'Come, Words, Away.'

In Part V the book is brought to an anti-poetic climax with the majestically didactic 'The Signs of Knowledge' and the eponymous 'Poet: A Lying Word' before subsiding into the measured prayer-cum-blessing of 'Benedictory Close' and the admonitory morning-after reflections of 'Apocryphal Numbers.' And then, after the nuclear season that 'should be winter but is not' we have poking through the ruins *The First Leaf* and *The Second Leaf.*

Amidst all the sound and fury of these major poems are serene and beautiful little poems which appear as if condensed like dew out of the atmosphere of her thought: 'Earth', 'With the Face' and 'The Flowering Urn.' These are poems which are attractive at first reading, but do not readily yield their concentrated meaning without reference to their wider context. A close reading of 'With the Face' is given as an appendix to this edition of the poems.

5

Following up on this first read-through we can begin again with the introductory poem 'As to a Frontispiece' which opens with the lines: 'If you will choose the portrait,|I will write the work accordingly.' After considering the alternatives of a 'German countenance' and a 'tidy creature, perhaps American' the poet reveals that

> I have a work but, I regret,
> No preliminary portrait
> And if you can forego one,
> We might between us illustrate
> This posthumous identity.[23]

For all its humour and apparent casualness the poem can be seen to introduce several threads that are woven through the subsequent poems. One of them is the idea of companionship and conversation, implicit here in the suggestion that collaboration between reader and poet/poem may be possible, indeed necessary, in order to illustrate 'This posthumous identity'. The reader is quite often addressed directly in the poems that follow, while 'The Courtesies of Authorship' and 'Poet: A Lying Word' focus on the nature of the relationship between reader and poet and/or poem in an unusually intense way.

'This posthumous identity' introduces a second thread: the suggestion of poetic immortality-in-death. Riding's use of the word 'death' to indicate what is final and immutable has exasperated and confounded some critics.[24] The word frequents her poems; here 'posthumous', with its derivation from the Latin for 'after burial in earth', suggests a subtle link with the word 'Earth', as in the poem of that title (which is fifth in the opening sequence). Her use of the word 'Earth' or 'earth', while seemingly figurative, is most helpfully read as 'literal on a large scale' as she herself says of her use of the word 'woman' referred to above. The word is both amplified and concentrated in the poems of the book. It is amplified in *Laura and Francisca*, where it is used to describe the journey inward:

> For death's a now like earth on which you stand
> And only readable by looking near ....
> Which closes up the eye? Then how to see? [...]
>
> Then where am I [...]
> I lie from Deyá inward by true leagues
> Of earthliness from the sun and sea
> Turning inward to nowhere-on-earth.[25]

The association of 'earth' with 'death' is plain in the most explicit (and outwardly bizarre and unpoetic) poem of her cosmogony, 'The Signs of Knowledge' where the second of the two signs (the first being 'unlove of the sun') is 'unlife of the earth', a phrase repeated three more times for the avoidance of doubt! These uses of 'earth' help us to understand the more concentrated use in the poem 'Earth' itself which begins 'Have no wide fears for Earth:|Its universal name is 'Nowhere' and climaxes in a yet bolder statement at the end of the poem:

> Earth is your heart
> Which has become your mind
> But still beats ignorance
> Of all it knows—
> As present miles deny the compact man
> Whose self-mistrusting past they are.
> Have no wide fears for Earth:
> Destruction on wide fears shall fall only.[26]

So the use of 'Earth' or 'earth' is complex, but if we return to 'posthumous' the simplest meaning is that, in completing the poem, it is 'dead' in Riding's special and paradoxical use of the word.

A third thread is the subtle play of appearance, or portraiture, against identity. The poems repeatedly ask the question: 'Who or what am I?' In one sense the whole of her poetry is a gigantic or minuscule self-portrait, one moment microcosmic the next macrocosmic in scale. There are glimpses of self-portraiture, of what in later life she entitled 'The Person I Am', throughout her poems.[27] In some of her poems before *Poet: A Lying Word* we can envisage the girl-poet thinking, as in 'Herself' (in 'Forgotten Girlhood'), dreaming in 'Incarnations', and resisting furious anger in 'Because I Sit Here So'. There is also 'Pride of Head' in which she describes her physical self, only twenty-three lines in *Collected Poems*, but a poem of seven sections ('Hair', 'Head Itself', 'Forehead', 'Eyes', 'Nose', 'Ears', and 'Mouth') covering eight pages of *The Close Chaplet*.[28] The portrayal may appear quite general to her gender, and may often be masked by mythical personae, as in 'Chloe Or ...', but as the poems progress the portrayal becomes more personal, as in 'The Tiger', more direct, as in 'The Rugged Black of Anger'. In the poem in which she contemplated suicide, 'In Nineteen Twenty-Seven', the 'I' who asks 'Then where was I, of this time and my own|A double ripeness and perplexity?' could be none other than Laura Riding.

In *Poet: A Lying Word* 'After Smiling' reads like a self-portrait of the author. In particular the second stanza, beginning 'Now is my smile pursed smooth|Into a stillest anger on|All flesh convivial' could be illustrated by the forbidding portrait of her by John Aldridge in 1933, contemporary with the first publication of the poem in *Poet: A Lying Word* and printed on the cover of this edition. While objecting to the thinness of her lips in the picture she described the portrait as 'a very good murderous-looking one.'[29] The stanza reads:

> Now is my smile pursed smooth
> Into a stillest anger on
> All flesh convivial
> To my convivial flesh
> Like scattered selves of me
> Insisting right of scatteredness
> And homed identity both—

As if by smiling promised.
The brilliant phrasing of 'Like scattered selves of me|Insisting
right of scatteredness|And homed identity both' is just one example
of the clarity and complexity of thought that Riding could achieve
in poetry.

6

Riding's poetry is as unique for what it renounces as for what it
espouses. As early as 1928 , in *Anarchism Is Not Enough*, she gave
hostages to those who would denigrate her poetry for its austerity
by denouncing regularity in rhythm and rhyme, and criticising 'false
critical analogies between poetry and music.' In particular, and in
direct contradiction of prevalent poetic values, she rejected the idea
that poetry should aim to have an emotional or a pleasant effect:

> The end of poetry is not to create a physical condition
> which shall give pleasure to the mind. It appeals to an
> energy in which no distinction exists between physical
> and mental conditions. It does not massage, soothe,
> excite or entertain this energy in any way. It *is* this
> energy in a form of extraordinary strength and intactness.[30]

At the same time there are outbreaks throughout the collection of
virtuoso eloquence. A few examples are given below:

> The body swimming in itself
> Is dissolution's darling—
> With dripping mouth it speaks a truth
> That cannot lie, in words not born yet
> Out of first immortality,
> All-wise impermanence.
> (From 'There is No Land Yet')

> Then open the small secret doors
> When none's there to read awrong.
> Out runs happiness in a crowd,
> The saving words and hours
> That come too tragic-late for souls

Gifted with their own mercy:
Denying that to themselves
Which never could be a joy,
Too orthodox maturity
For such heresy of child-remaining.
On these the grey-beard pleasures of books fall—
Pink, pundit babyhood
Whose blinking vision stammers out
A blind big-lettered foetus-future.
   (From 'Unread Pages')

Goodbye, I cannot bring you closer
If you prefer the ghostly way,
Keeping the living side of death.
Not I you sat with, but a pathos,
My partial image torn out of me.
Nor ever will you have me whole.
   (From 'It is not Sad')

And to make no mistake, write *Poison* on me,
To know the bottle which,
And notify your sick distrust of sweet.
Have you an appetite for death now?
Never, never, need that lack,
Self-cheated Ghost, with memory where your head
And pain where once your heart—
You own credulity's fool.
And the bones, the sceptic corpse
That you stood up from doubting stone?
They grind the death of vanity, found long ago,
And have no death of will to ask now:
Let them to earth again, like roots torn up
With flower along that never dreamed of vase.
   (From 'As to Food')

When's man a poet then? And was he ever one?
And if a death with that slow instant stays
That is no instant, when the frightened flesh
Runs hard after the blood fleeing homeward
To previous courses and reddened turns—
That's none of him, no part forgotten,
But of his second love a fancy
Lying man-like in her fancied arms [....]

The man's away after the man.
She understood his wooing wrong.
He never meant her more than paper,
Nor does his shivering heart one icy line remember [...]
(From 'Two Loves, One Madness')

My eyes, my mouth, my hovering hands, my
intransmutable head: wherein my eyes, my mouth, my
hands, my head, my body-self, are not such mortal
simulacrum as everlong you builded against very death, to
keep you everlong in boasted deathcourse, neverlong? I say,
I say, I am not builded of you so.
(From 'Poet: A Lying Word')

If I my words am,
If the footed head which frowns them
And the handed heart which smiles them
Are this very table, chair,
This paper, pencil, taut community
Wherein enigma's orb is word-constrained.
Does myself upon the page meet,
Does the thronging firm a name
To nod my own— witnessing
I write or am this— it is written?
What thinks the world?
Has here the time-eclipsed occasion

Grown language-present?
(From *The Second Leaf*)

Towards the end of her life, long after her renunciation 'of allegiance to poetry as a profession and faith in it as an institution', in a commentary on her making occasional use of a 'poetic form of pronouncement' she remarked:

> I give way in these instances to a free-will impulsion to take advantage of the special potency of poetic speech as allowing a forceful avoidance of the delay in communicative advance, the circuitous linguistic spaciousness of which prose allows. This potency inheres in poetry.[31]

The lines of poems quoted above give examples of that potency in practice.

7

Riding's poetry and her thought generally, lack sentimentality about 'nature'. In her *Collected Poems* there is not a single poem 'identifying' with a bird or animal as Blake did in 'The Fly', for example:

> Am not I
> A fly like thee?
> Or art not thou
> A man like me?

This may seem harmless enough but there is the danger that poets 'lose themselves' in this kind of anthropomorphism, or pathetic fallacy, which sees humanity in nature. Some of Ted Hughes' animal poems take this to an extreme. Several of Riding's poems in this volume oppose, and indeed can be said to reverse anthropomorphism, good examples being 'Intelligent Prayer', 'Short of Strange', and 'Tree-Sense'. On first reflection the pathetic fallacy and anthropomorphism may seem easy targets, but Riding's real criticism is of poets whose *aim* (not just their achievement) falls short of our full human capacity and potential for truth.

Lyricism has had of course sweet ['humane' in *CP*]
                                                              use in time:

To allow the bragging population to recover
From the exertion of behaving intelligently
By intelligencing the unintelligence
Of stupid darlings also prone to think,
Though in such cases minds are only leaves, or less.
                    (From 'Intelligent Prayer')

But to change to flies—
To perhaps not strange flies,
They which so prettily annoy
And with regret
See themselves killed,
Scarcely alive, scarcely dead.
Or of moths, how if turned outdoors
Next morning with goodbye,
A gratitude beyond their will
Humanizes the unasked release,
And an emotion reels away.
Such insincere hysterias
Or terrorless philosophies
Show nature's suave proficiency in man.
                    (From 'Short of Strange')

Our humility before 'nature' (as, it might be added, our humility before 'God') is a false humility, it amounts to a shirking of our task and our opportunity, described by Riding in her first poetic credo in 1925.[32] For her the prime mover is the poet, the creator is him (or her, of course):

Life is create with him. The poetry of this mood will have still
the wonder, still the exaltation. But the wonder will proceed

not from the accidental contacts with a life that comes to us as a visitation but from a sense of self that adventures so steadfastly, so awarely beyond it that its discoveries have the character of creation and the eternal element of self-destiny.

[...] For this poetry, song is not surrender but salvation.

As with (the traditional poetic stance toward) nature so with (the traditional stance toward) God or gods. In the second poem in the book, the beautifully simple and direct 'There are as Many Questions as Answers' she wrote:

What is to be?
It is to bear a name.
What is to die?
It is to be name only.
And what is to be born?
It is to choose the enemy self
To learn impossibility from.
What is it to have hope?
Is it to choose a god weaker than self,
And pray for compliments?

For her there was no detachment. Her poetry affects, even overturns, our world view. We cannot remain detached and enjoy it 'as poetry', because its implications are so uncomfortable. If it is true, it changes us.

Endnotes

1 Jack Blackmore *The Unthronged Oracle* (Cirencester: Mereo, 2016).

2 W. H. Auden's career was launched by wholesale 'borrowing' from her poems in 1930 and his famous later line, in 'In Memory of W.B. Yeats' that 'poetry makes nothing happen' is a watered down version of Riding's radical and serious thought in the short essay 'What is a Poem?': 'What is a poem? A poem is nothing. By persistence the poem can be made into something; but then it is something, not a poem. [...] It is not an effect (common or uncommon) of experience); it is the result of an ability to create

a vacuum in experience.' *An-archism Is Not Enough*, (London: Cape, 1928), 16-17.

This crystalline thought has meandered into mainstream thought. Charles Bernstein, for example, repeats the thought, unacknowledged, in a recent interview in the Internet literary journal *Rail*. However 'poetry makes nothing happen' is not what LR means. She means that it makes *nothing* happen, it creates an implosion, creates a hole in 'our' reality.

John Ashbery confessed to relying on her for his first collection of poems. And then there is the more serious case of Robert Graves who depended on her ideas which he misapplied in his own poetry and prose. Initially he fully acknowledged his dependence, but later made every effort to distance himself.

Relevant essays on Riding's influence are Michael Kirkham, 'Robert Graves's Debt to Laura Riding', *Focus on Robert Graves*, 3 (December 1973), 33-44; Philip Rowland, '"Celebration of Failure": The Influence of Laura Riding on John Ashbery', at *www.flashpointmag.com/riding.htm* (accessed 6th Feb 2017). Ironically Graves himself wrote a letter to Auden complaining about his taking of lines of Riding's poems to incorporate into his own, an accusation he repeated in his Clark Lectures in 1954-55: 'I had to suggest that the half-guinea he paid for Laura Riding's *Love as Love, Death as Death* gave him no right to borrow half lines and whole lines from them for insertion in his own verse.' *The Crowning Privilege* (London: Penguin, 1959), 151.

3 There is a line by line analysis of this poem (and other poems derived from *PALW*, including 'Come, Words, Away', 'Bishop Modernity', 'Earth' and 'The Flowering Urn') in my *The Unthronged Oracle* (Cirencester: Mereo, 2016).

4 The intensive and restless process by which Riding reworked her poems can be illustrated by reviewing the various versions of what was 'In Memory of Friends' in *Twenty Poems Less* (Paris: Hours Press, 1930), 20. The next version became almost unrecognizable, apart from the final lines, as 'War Ways' in *PALW* (1933) and was then again mostly rewritten as 'Regret of War Ways' in *Collected Poems* (1938), 158.

5 The four prose works I refer to are: Laura Riding, *Four Unposted Letters to Catherine* (Paris: Hours Press, 1930); Laura Riding, *Experts Are Puzzled* (London: Cape, 1930); 'Barbara Rich' (one of Riding's pen-names), *No Decency*

Left (L ondon: Cape, 1932); Laura Riding (editor and arranger), *Everybody's Letters* (London: Arthur Barker, 1933).

6 Joyce Piell Wexler, *Laura Riding's Pursuit of Truth* (Athens: Ohio University Press, 1979), 73. I have used a colon (as opposed to the comma Wexler uses) in the title of *Poems: A Joking Word* as this is how it appeared on the dustcover of Poet: A Lying Word. On the cover of the book itself (and inside) there is no punctuation, just '*Poems*' in italics, followed by 'A Joking Word' in plain type.

7 Interestingly even Robert Nye, a lifetime devotee of Riding's poems, included only ten of the poems from *Poet: A Lying Word* in his otherwise generous selection, which had by contrast eighteen of her earliest poems from her *First Awakenings*, edited by Elizabeth Friedmann, Alan J. Clark and Robert Nye (Manchester: Carcanet, 1992) which the author had excluded altogether from her *Collected Poems*. Laura Riding, *A Selection of the Poems of Laura Riding*, edited with an introduction by Robert Nye (Manchester: Carcanet, 1994). He even omits what to me is one of the finest short poems in the language, 'With the Face'.

8 'Excerpts From A Recording (1972), Explaining The Poems'. Published as Appendix V in *The Poems of Laura Riding*, the centenary edition of *Collected Poems* (2001), (New York: Persea Books, 2001), with a preface by Mark Jacobs and a note on the text by Alan Clark, 496.

9 The two separate parts of what became 'Disclaimer of the Person' in *Collected Poems* were first published as unbound sheets *Th e Fi rst Leaf* (Majorca: The Seizin Press, 1933) and *The Second Leaf* (Majorca: The Seizin Press, 1935). The original titles are ironically suggestive of an aftermath following the 'season that should be winter but is not'. However the first and second leaf are not of another spring of 'green and tangled nature' but of her own determined continuance to in composing (on single sheets or 'leaves' of paper). See too the next note on 'poems as the most important forms of life.'

10 In the notes of her interesting little anthology Gwendolen Murphy wrote of Riding (no doubt with her approval, probably quoting her) that she 'regards poems as the most important form of life'. In writing *The Unthronged Oracle* I overlooked the notes written by Riding for the anthology on her view of what a poem is, and also important notes to individual poems, notably those

on 'The Quids'. Gwendolen Murphy, *The Modern Poet* (London: Sidgwick & Jackson, 1938), 184-188.

11 'The Idea of God' first appeared in *Epilogue I* in 1935, but was reprinted reprinted in Laura Riding and Robert Graves, *Essays from Epilogue 1935-1937*, edited with an introduction by Mark Jacobs (Manchester: Carcanet, 2001), 5-37. Laura (Riding) Jackson, *The Word "Woman"*, edited by Elizabeth Friedmann and Alan J. Clark (New York: Persea Books, 1993).

12 Points of comparison suggest themselves at various points: Coleridge's reference to the 'despotism of the eye'; his idea of the mind being made in 'the Image of the Creator' and not a 'lazy Looker-on on an external world'; his systematic 'desynonymization' of words such as 'fancy' and 'imagination'; the idea that 'A Poet's *Heart & Intellect* should be *combined, intimately* combined & *unified*, with the great appearances in nature – & not merely held in solution & loose mixture with them, in the shape of formal Similies [*sic*].' (All quoted from John Spencer-Hill, *Imagination in Coleridge* [London: Macmillan, 1978], 6, 21, 109, 23). It could be argued that Riding is a radical and intrepid successor to Coleridge. She herself notes some correspondences (but characteristically also differences) between her and Coleridge in her 'Addendum' to *The Telling* (London: Athlone, 1972), 179-85. Riding's reported view is given in Murphy (1938), 186 (see Note 10).

13 'Excerpts From A Recording (1972), Explaining The Poems' in the cente-nary edition of *Collected Poems* (2001), 496-97. She goes on to discountenance utterly the 'goddess notioning' which Graves developed into the widely-hailed book, *The White Goddess*, which influenced Plath and Hughes, amongst others.

14 Quotations taken from two separate passages in 'To the Reader':
   'One reads to uncover to oneself something that would otherwise
   remain unknown —something that one feels it is important to know.'
   A poem is an uncovering of truth of so fundamental and general
   kind that no other name besides poetry is adequate except truth.'
Collected Poems (London: Cassell, 1938), xvi and xviii; reprinted in *The Poems of Laura Riding, a Newly Revised Edition of the 1938 and 1980 Collection (New York: Persea Books, 2001)* 483 and 484.

15 'In Nineteen Twenty-Seven', where the continuation makes clear that she is in her own time: 'Then, where was I, of this time and my own|A double ripeness and perplexity?|Fresh year of time, desire,|Late year of my age, renunciation.'

16 Laura Riding and Robert Graves, *A Survey of Modernist Poetry* (London: Heinemann, 1927); these quotations are taken from the reprinted edition of Riding and Graves, *A Survey of Modernist Poetry* and *A Pamphlet Against An-thologies* (Manchester: Carcanet, 2002), 129, 130.

17 An observation I owe to Mark Jacobs. See his essay 'Contemporary Misogyny: Laura Riding, William Empson and the Critics: A Survey of Mis-History' in *English*, 2015, which unravels the sorry history of misattribution of the credit for the authorship of *A Survey*.

18 *Contemporaries And Snobs* (London: Cape, 1928) 10.

19 *Anarchism Is Not Enough* (London: Cape, 1928). The essays most relevant to Riding's vision of poetry are in the first half of the book, pages 9-132. See also my account of the relevance of her essay 'Poetry and Music' in *The Unthronged Oracle* (2016), 13-16.

20 From the chapter 'Variety in Modernist Poetry'. This remark quite probably suggested Ted Hughes' comments (brilliantly satirized by Wendy Cope in 'A Policeman's Lot'): 'The progress of any writer is marked by those moments when he manages to outwit his own inner police system.'

The remarks on gentility remind one of Riding's own background. Her father was a working man, and a passionate socialist. Although Riding's political views were very different she retained great respect for him.

21 *A Survey of Modernist Poetry* (2002), 96.

22 These are some of the definitions of 'peculiar' given in O.E.D.

23 *Poet: A Lying Word* (London: Arthur Barker, 1933), 3. The first published version, in *Twenty Poems Less* (Paris: Hours Press, 1930), 1, was substantially revised for *PALW*, the last three lines quoted replacing the blander 'And if you could forego one| We might arrive, pending your pleasure| At some not inapt compromise.' These final three lines were altered again in *Collected Poems* to 'Yet, if you can forego one,| We may between us illustrate| This subsequent identity.'

24 Joyce Wexler's *Laura Riding: A Bibliography* (New York: Garland, 1981) provides an invaluable and fascinating selection of reviews in the section 'Writings About Laura Riding' (117-154). It is far from comprehensive however. For example Wexler cites only one review of *PALW*, that of the *Times Literary Supplement* in 1934, with a negative conclusion: "But we are left wondering, noting her skill, what weariness or accident has turned her from the objective sensuous world of poetry to explore the inarticulate deserts, which she calls death." (Wexler, 1981, 126). In her biography, by contrast, Elizabeth Friedmann managed to find and to quote from six other contemporary reviews of *PALW*, five of them positive (*A Mannered Grace* [New York: Persea Books, 2005)], 217-18).

25 *PALW*, 116, 117.

26 *PALW*, 11. Amended in *Collected Poems* so that the fifth line reads 'As miles deny the compact present', and the last is the rather more elegant 'Destruction only on wide fears shall fall'.

27 Chapter 1 of Volume 1 of *The Person I Am* (Trent Editions: Nottingham Trent University, 2011), 48.

28 The poem is called 'Body's Head' in *The Close Chaplet* (New York: Adelphi, 1926), 21-28. 'Pride of Head' is adapted from the second section of 'Body's Head', entitled 'Head Itself'. The poem reminds me of the examination of Gulliver by the Lilliputians.

29 The quote is taken from Elizabeth Friedmann's biography, *A Mannered Grace* (New York: Persea Books, 2005), 203. There is a good discussion by Friedmann of the two contrasting portraits of Riding (the other being by Arnold Mason), both painted in 1933, at pp208-09.

30 In 'Poetry and Music' in *Anarchism Is Not Enough* (London: Cape, 1928), 34-35. A full account of this essay is given in my *The Unthronged Oracle* (2016), chapter 1.

31 Laura (Riding) Jackson in conversation with Elizabeth Friedmann, *PN Review*, March April 1991, 74.

32 'A Prophecy or a Plea', *The Reviewer*, 5(2), April 1925, 1-7. Reproduced in Laura Riding, *First Awakenings: The Early Poems* (Manchester: Carcanet, 1992), 275-280, quotation from 279.

A Note on the Text

The text of the original edition has been completely reset. The pages are slightly longer and wider in this new edition, which has the effect of altering the numbering. This potential disadvantage is offset by the fact that several more of the poems now appear on a single page, and that most of the longer lines no longer need to be broken. In some cases where it is unclear whether or not a stanza break should coincide with a new page, reference has been made to other printed versions of the poem in question, in particular the author's *Collected Poems*, but it is not always possible to be conclusive.

Obvious errors have been corrected, including a superfluous full stop in the title of 'There are as Many Questions as Answers', and misprints/misspellings of 'impossibility' in that poem, of 'indecision' in the poem 'War Ways' and 'identical' in the poem 'Tree Sense'.

There is an anomaly in respect of the title of the poem 'Who', as noted by Wexler in her bibliography. On the contents page it is accompanied by a question mark, whereas above the poem itself it appears without one. The anomaly is not entirely resolved by reference to the earlier version of the poem in *Twenty Poems Less* (Paris: Hours Press, 1930) where on the contents page the title appears as 'Who' and above the poem itself it is 'Whose', neither with a question mark. However, in *Collected Poems* the poem is entitled simply 'Who' on both contents page and above the poem itself, and it has been amended thus in this new edition.

As noted in the introduction, two poems not in the original book, *The First Leaf* (1933) and *The Second Leaf* (1935), have been included as an addendum. The two poems were originally published by the Seizin Press, as separate sheets, copies of which are now very rare. Thematic justification for their inclusion here is that in Riding's *Collected Poems* they were included, combined into one two-part poem, entitled 'Disclaimer of the Person', at the end of the section 'Poems of Final Occasion' — the rest of that section being made up of poems from *Poet: A Lying Word*.

PART I

SHREWD WINTER, AND THE LAST:
THE NEXT YEAR STANDS STILL

AS TO A FRONTISPIECE

If you will choose the portrait,
I will write the work accordingly.
A German countenance
I could dilate on lengthily,
Punctilio and passion blending
To that slow national degree.

Or, if you wish more brevity
And have the face in mind—
A tidy creature, perhaps American—
I could provide a facile text,
The portrait being like enough
To stand for anyone.

But if you can't make up your mind
What poetry should look like,
What name to call for,
I think I have the very thing
If you can read without a picture
And postpone the frontispiece till later.

That is, as you may guess,
I have a work but, I regret,
No preliminary portrait.
And if you can forgo one,
We might between us illustrate
This posthumous identity.

THERE ARE AS MANY QUESTIONS AS ANSWERS

What is to start?
It is to have feet to start with.
What is to end?
It is to have nothing to start again with,
And not to wish.

What is to see?
It is to know in part.
What is to speak?
It is to add part to part
And make a whole
Of much or little.
What is to whisper?
It is to make soft
The greed of speaking faster
Than is substance for.
What is to cry out?
It is to make gigantic
Where speaking cannot last long.

What is to be?
It is to bear a name.
What is to die?
It is to be name only.
And what is to be born?
It is to choose the enemy self
To learn impossibility from.
And what is it to have hope?
Is it to choose a god weaker than self,
And pray for compliments?

What is to ask?
It is to find an answer.
And what is to answer?
Is it to find a question?

THE FACT

While discovery is the fact,
Sea-skill and the way to find,
Flee, land, more inland,
Even to the Devil's bosom, loneliness.

Which cannot comfort,
But which cannot give a foreign name
Or make you other than desolate.

Yet be not undiscoverable,
Except where land seen is mere sailor's fancy,
Not native strangeness.

For if you be a true unknown,
Discovery must fade into you
And the foreign name translate.

And the discoverer succeed the Devil,
Even unto loneliness—
To comfort by it,
By it call you known.

AND I

And I,
And do I ask,
How long this pain?
Do I not show myself in every way
To be happy in what most ravages?

When I have grown old in these delights,
Then usedness and not exclaiming
May well seem unenthusiasm.

But now, how am I delicate?
Wherein do I prefer
The better to the worse?

I will tell you.
There is a passing fault in her:
To be mild in my very fury.
And ' Beloved ' she is called.
And pain I hunt alone,
While she hangs back smiling
And lets flattery crowd her round—
As if I hunted insult not true love.

But how may I be hated
Unto true love's all of me?
I will tell you.
The fury will grow into calm
As I grow into her
And, smiling always,
She looks serenely on their death-struggles,
Having looked serenely on mine.

EARTH

Have no wide fears for Earth:
Its universal name is 'Nowhere'.
If it is Earth to you, that is your secret.
The outer records leave off there,
And you may write it as it seems,
And as it seems, it is,
A seeming stillness
Amidst seeming speed.

Heavens unseen, or only seen,
Dark or light space, unearthly space,
Is a time before Earth was
From which you inward move
Toward perfect now.

Almost the place it is not,
Potential here of everywhere—
Have no wide fears for earth:
Its destiny is simple,
To be further what it is.

Earth is your heart
Which has become your mind
But still beats ignorance
Of all it knows—
As present miles deny the compact man
Whose self-mistrusting past they are.
Have no wide fears for Earth:
Destruction on wide fears shall fall only.

UNLESS INFINITY IS ONLY TIME

Greater is to lesser
As many is to one—
Breaths of breath.

An infinity of lack describes
The indescribable moment of enough.
And this is not comparison,
Only a proved equality
Of much and little.

Nor even nothingness
Impossible to sum,
Unless infinity but a waning is
Rather than to add up slowly
The one and one and one
That nothingness of one makes millionish—
Unless infinity is only time
And thinks the moment to outnumber
Which indeed weightless keeps the scales
In such eternal balance
Of unnumbered one against
The moment upon moment that bears down,
In mathematical spite
Or fond amazement, the other way.

THE JUDGEMENT

The judgement is prepared.
In every respect it is exact and just.
Then why no doom,
Why no deliverance?

The judgement is prepared,
It was prepared,
It never failed to be,
Should ever the rightful cause
Speak at the rightful bar—
A coincidence that has not yet astounded,
Or one so close that it did not astound
And properly now afterwards
Runs on as now before.

And properly some in agitation go,
As if the very end were,
And some in dullard peace,
As if it ever had been,
And some in artfulness,
As if it had or had not,
Both and either, which or which.
And properly, however,
The judgement being fixed
In every multiplied respect,
And clear in every separate article,
Though as the silence of a written voice
In its full utterance.

EGYPT

Egypt, premortuary tomb where
Conscience of death makes dead, and great
In natal flesh given to this grandeur,
To Vanity the foster-death,
The glamorous erosion—
And who does not lie there,
A mummy not yet born?
Who does not lie there,
Who lives?
Except the Devil and his numbers
The upper air usurping
While the great dead still sleep?

But when the great dead at last live,
What is Egypt then?
When Nefertiti is fairer than a queen
And the lachrymatory vessels are full
In the name not of buried sorrow?

Egypt is then the Devil's pit of pride,
Where, counterfeiting immortality,
The angry souls that never risked name
Lie down in jealous triumph of will
And dream of grandeur never lost
To the true grandeur and death.

THE WAY IT IS

It falls to an idiot to talk wisely.
It falls to a sot to wear beauty.
It falls to many to be blessed
In their shortcomings,
As to the common brute it falls
To see real miracles
And howl with irksome joy.

Many are the confusions that fall,
Many are the inspired ones.
Much is there indeed contrary,
Much is there indeed wonderful.
A most improbable one it takes
To tell what is so,
And the strangest creature of men
To be his natural self.

WHO

But whose house or head
Or intimate or ruling presence?
Am I by a ticket of identity,
Like any other lifetime?
But suppose no house or head
Or actuality called mine?
Then am I by a broomstick
As when I rode and was not,
Unlike any other lifetime.

The answer concerns you, I think,
Your prosperity, not mine.
When you could spare me but a broomstick,
You were but a poor world
That must grudge me even a broomstick.
Now you are bolder to possess yourselves,
And I am nearly what I am,
As nearly as I may be
In a generous world of others.

WE

We, the befallen fates,
We are known and necessitous
To all but the children.
And to them we are words.
We are death, not befallen.
We are justice, not swift.
We are knowledge, not ominous.

And their mother is a meanwhile.
She teaches them the game self,
How to spin out suspense
By a winner and a next game:
While we, the fates to befall,
Keep our same watch, unpredictableness.

To the children is given a mother,
To make them strong in days.
To the mother is given a dark spirit.
He brings the nights on.
From sweet light to sweet hell
Runs the story that softens
Death, the true story.

To the mother is given a lover,
Time gives the demon Future.
But the father is the immediate
Angel of impatience.
Her very womb is a man.
And she is but a meanwhile.

And the children are but a never.
And we are but the last present

From which date back all presents
To the past of all meanwhiles—
An order of shortcoming
Rising into never-us
Like children agedly prolonging childhood.

FURTHER DETAILS

The reward of curiosity
In such as you are
(Statisticians of doubt)
Is increased cause for curiosity.
And the punishment thereof,
To be not a cat.

I shall inform you truthfully,
And you will hear philosophically,
And more words will be required,
And you shall have them.

There is no end of information
Where there is no end of intelligence
By which to comprehend
Always somewhat.

As through a stained-glass vision
The simple instantaneous light
Is gradual and shy as God.

That is, as much remains to be described
As you have ear for.
And you have not only a live ear
But an immortal mind.

Assuming by your finical attention
That you allow the whole and ask
A mere enumeration of parts,
I shall avoid all argument.
In the general thing, we agree.
In the particulars, you are well-disposed.

I shall pay you the humane compliment
Of not beginning at the beginning—
Which is the procedure with cats.
May you be long in dying.
Is this not your wish?

WAR WAYS

Can friends grow strange?
Can love make history?
But they have all my love now
Which before was halved with enemies.

And love is much.
They weary of me.
I am like peace embracing
Who have no heart but to be brave.

The happy days of war,
Is their regret,
When they more tasted of my enemies
Than this unarguable me.

Vanished into variety
Those hosts of indecision
That in the gracious name of faith
They hotly persecuted.

And, loyal to vexedness,
They fret away my too whole presence:
Then to mourn me without grief,
As ghosts mourn the living.

THE COURTESIES OF AUTHORSHIP

Now that you have read of,
You will want to see.
I can only take you to the place
And let you not see.
Then you may choose freely
Between my book and your eye.
You will undoubtedly prefer your eye,
To not see for yourself.
I shall be delighted to withdraw my book
In favour of your however blind eye.
But I will not withdraw my book
In favour of any book of yours,
In favour of time-begging prophecy.
This may be still an early hour for seeing,
But it is a late hour for telling of.
And I will not be indistinct
That the confounded may distribute
Confusion like a cheaper gold....
I have a bargain too to drive:
Here's nothing you need fear to do without
So long the price of it remains unspent
For the time when a decent shroud
To cover ignorance of death
Is offered against knowledge no more for sale—
Else naked must you go then,
A fool exposed and nothing to buy shame with,
Squandered the discreet gold of patience
On promised visions, sworn imaginary,
Nor any hope of suicide or murder left,
You being already dead, and all the brusque immortals.

50

THEN FOLLOWS

Then follows a description
Of an interval called death
By the living.
But I shall speak of it
As of brief illness.
For it lasted only
From being not ill
To being not ill.

It came about by chance—
I met God.
'What,' he said, ' you already?'
'What,' I said, 'you still?'
He apologized and I apologized.
'I thought I was alone,' he said.
'Are you displeased?' I said.
'I suppose I should not be,' he said.
A dove hopped out of his sleeve
And muted well in his palm.
Frowning, he wrung its neck.
'Are there any more of you?' he said,
Tears in his eyes, but politely.
'As many as you care to meet,' I said.
Tears falling, he said politely,
'I can't wait, but remember me to them.'

Here was an awkward moment
Worthy of my awkwardness at last.
For my remaining always same and self-like
In scenes of certain unreality—
Or at least no quick likeness to what's gone before—
Is no mere want of grace.

A Prince once kissed my cheek, saying,
'Accept the only homage possible
From a vulgarian.'
And I did not protest.
But that was in a dream,
And the fellow only democratic-royal.
This was a more far-reaching
Crisis of deportment,
And I am describing it
Without lightness or guile.
Indeed, my manner at the time
Was my manner now.

Then God said, 'I suppose I must be going.'
I said, not impolitely, 'I suppose you must.'
Then follows a description
Of this brief illness,
Not to seem to be saying idly,
'I am not ill,' which of course you knew.

Yes, there has been an interval
Generally described as death.
Thank you, I am now as I was.
Perhaps you are not really interested,
Since it was really only a brief illness.
But I think it right to tell you
That nothing worse can happen now—
It was the worst, and thank you.
Then follows the old routine
Of being, thank you, not ill.
Perhaps, like God, you had better be going,
Instead of tears, a bored expression,
It having been made clear to you

That no more may be expected of me
Than to be as usual not ill.
Think of me, if you like, as dead,
And no description following.

And if this seems too final,
Was such not our common object,
Although our meanings differ somewhat,
Yours being of the book,
Mine of myself?
You were listening for a something
And I have uttered you a something
That further listening of yours
And further uttering of mine
Could not make mean to you
More than you wished to know
Of what comes after—
Not more than: here ends.

My progress is not, like yours,
Toward a last page.
Ought we not part therefore when you tire
And make as if not to turn over?
For my progress is toward
To be as usual not ill.
A description having followed
Of an interval called death
By the living,
Perhaps you had better be going,
Since you have not my way of talking.
There is always difference somewhat
When meanings differ somewhat.
You would continue to wear
A look of waiting for

A chapter that you'ld never read.
And I to seem only standing still
Between furthermore and furthermore.
You would complain much of the weather,
That everybody's scapegoat.

What, you may say,
Have I grown cold to you,
Have we not been friends since—
Yes, since the first page.
No, I am as usual,
Sensitive to the weather, like you,
Yet not bewitched in it.
But you are growing different,
Querulously obsessed with day on day.
By your time, the same as mine
When once we had one clock,
Patience is threadbare.
By mine, I am as usual not ill
After a brief illness,
An interval upon which
Verbal unanimity divides.

You wished to learn courage
For a certain destined major event
By flattering me to go first.
But, being not of your long ranks
Of time-strung distances from truth,
I have been here always
And so have only to report
A certain chance minor event
That fell to me by irony alone
Of walking into where I was.
At least, I cannot teach you courage,

Which comes by the grace of God
When patience goes.
I am not God.
True, we have met,
Which seems to spell identity,
Since God like me went first.
But that will always be
To-morrow to God,
As it has always been
A yesterday to me
Between to-day and to-day.

And now I shall be frank,
Since we are about to part.
The interval, a description of which
Followed your desire for one,
Was a description merely.
I have not, of course, met God,
Or been ill, either long or briefly.
What, I have lied to you!
Yes, I have lied.
And, having had your lie,
Perhaps now you had better be going.
Then follows all that has preceded.
No, I have not met God.
Or, if you insist upon the truth,
I have so met him.
And what now, having had your truth?
Perhaps you will not be going.
Clearly some one had better be going.
I, for one, shall continue where I am.
God, I believe, will live on memories,
You, I believe, each on forgetfulness.
Perhaps we had all better be going.

Or perhaps I have not made myself plain.

Ah, the pity of it for me,
To be by name a poet,
To make myself plain,
And yet not to make myself plain
Because of being by name a poet,
A creature neither man nor God.
Yes, such a creature by name,
And by nature like both man and God—
Like God, a creature of mind,
Like man, a creature of mouth.
Ah, the pity of it,
To be a creature of both mouth and mind,
But to be by name a poet,
As if a third order where but two struggled
Were the ambiguous peace thereof.

And ah, the pity of it for you,
To be by nature man or by nature God,
And poet by name only to affirm
That beyond man and God lies only
Such beyond as poet alone can affirm,
Being creature of name only—
Ah, the pity of it for us all.
Perhaps we had better not be going.
Perhaps I had better write another poem
And, if necessary, yet another,
Until a description follows
Of an interval after which
There's no return to time again,
To paradoxing truth between
Two similar poles of human logic—
After which no description

Unless words have wordless echo
As sound derived of silence
Might break unheard against itself
And echo silently
Through infinite parabolas
Of no description following.

PART II

SPRING HOLDS THE PRESENT BACK

ALL THINGS

All things that wake enjoy the sun—
All things but one—
All things except the sun—
The sun because the sun.

An observation of my girlhood.
 I now speak less equivocally
And yet more guardedly.

All things that wake enjoy the sun—
All things but one—
All things except the sun—
The sun because
All things once sun were
Which more and more was
The pride that could not be
Except looked back on
By all things become
One, one and one
Unto death's long precision.

All things that wake enjoy the ,sun.
All things remember not having been,
When waking was but sun to be,
And sleeping was but sun to be,
When life was life alone once—
Deathless, all-instantaneous,
Begun and done in one
Impossibility of being sun,
Death's too proud enemy—
All things enjoy to watch
The pride that could not be,

The wholeness against death—
All things enjoy to watch this
From death where life is
As lasting as it little is.

An observation of my—
What shall I call such patience
To look back on nature,
Having already looked enough
To know the sun it is which was,
And the sun again which was not,
By nights removed from self,
By nights and days, by souls
Like little suns away toward
Dreams of pride that could not be—
What shall I call such patience—
An observation of my agedness—
Death's long precision while
All things undo themselves
From sunhood, living glory
That never, never was—
Because the sun.

LINES IN SHORT DESPITE OF TIME

Forgive me, giver, if I destroy the gift!
It is so nearly what would please me,
I cannot but perfect it.

*

' Worthy of a jewel', they say of beauty,
Uncertain what is beauty
And what the precious thing.

*

While the calendar still reads to-day,
Admire coldly: enthusiasm blears,
And makes death invisible.

*

And if occasionally a rhyme appeared,
This was the illness but not the death
So fear-awaited that hope of it
Ailing forgetfulness became.

*

Between the word and the world lie
Fading eternities of soon.

*

In short despite of time, that long despite of truth,
By all that's false and would be true as truth,
Here's truth in time, and false as false,
To say, ' Let all of us be one
In names so opposite, there's no
Long-short of it between us more.'

IF A POEM LASTS TWENTY-FOUR HOURS

Between the always coming revelation
And the proud crowd—
Proud to be crowd—
First crying, Speak!
(Thus cries dumbly self-loved nature
Or nature-plumed America)
Then smiling deafly
In blind enjoyment
Of that not flattering hour—
Between that word or hour
Or close determination on paper
And that perhaps world of witness,
Stands perhaps this female interlocutor.

She had a Spanish husband,
But I met the woman later,
When her judicating vision was
As colour-incorrect
As black-and-white my earth
Of unchromatic right and wrong,
And where the listening population
Was more of earth than nature.
Therefore our conversation
Was more of money than of art.
For money judicates,
But does not bandy love.

*

Of bandying love,
This is of children.
For who tells save somewhat
(Of those who know),
Who teaches all

(Of those who teach),
Down to destruction?

Of bandying love,
This is between the slow womb, the word,
And its hasty seed, its speaking—
Until between slowness and hastiness
There is no hastiness and slowness,
No more than between mother and man,
Between man and woman.

Who, then, is child,
And who is man?
Child is the first man still,
Man is the last man not yet.
And the first man is seed,
And the last man is seed silenced.
The last man is woman-wise:
Woman which before man
Was silent word alone—
That breeding silence she.

Let it be a care
How man or child
Be called man or child,
Or woman, woman.

*

Let it also be a care
To be whole by breaking and by mending.
The body is a day of ruin,
The mind, a moment of repair.
A day is not a day of mind
Until a lifetime is despair.
To break, to day-long die,

To be not yet nor yet
Until dreaming is of having been,
Until dreaming is of having dreamed—
How in those days—how fast—
How fast you seemed to dream—
How fast you talked—how lost—
How lost the words until—
Until the pen ran down
To this awakened not forgetting.

But in those days always
How forgotten—and to say over—
To say now and now—
Or in a letter to say over soon—

Do you remember now, John,
Our suburban conversation once of bees?
Neatly at breakfast we of bees,
A retired talk or walk
Among the outskirts of profundity?
Slowly of honeycombs and swarms
And angry queens we?

*

But slowly bees is briefest dozing.
Between the country and the city,
Between sound sleep and waking,
More gives to pause and buzz than bees
A short story in a—and by—
Nor need tastes differ but to pause.

Do you remember now, John,
Do you remember my friend John
Who had a lordly not-to-hurry eye,
A very previous eye

In an advanced socket?
Yes, I remember.
And I remember my friend Norman,
Though by frugality of will
He shall arrive punctually to-morrow
When even the cinematograph of time
Has ceased to advertise to-day—
Though I remember.

Yes, she remembers all that seemed,
All that was like enough to now
To make a then as actual as then,
To make a now that succeeds only
By a more close resemblance to itself.

MEANWHILE

Equally dismal rain and sunshine—
If the hours are hours of waiting
To say for certain You, and I.
Happily there is this sure We,
Happily there is this love,
This chosen ambiguity,
Until the weather knows its mind. . . .

Meanwhile this to-day,
To succeed never beyond the weather—
Until it climates death,
That ripened clarity
Of difference.

INTELLIGENT PRAYER

A star by world-connivance seems part of the hill.
A tree not by mere humour stands creature-like.
Such painstaking acts of intelligence widely accost.
It is a compliment to nature to perceive them.
The mind is already full and nearly breaking.
It is no mean compliment to stop and smile
And verse such imperfections perfectwise.

Lyricism has had of course sweet use in time:
To allow the bragging population to recover
From the exertion of behaving intelligently
By intelligencing the unintelligence
Of stupid darlings also prone to think,
Though in such cases minds are only leaves, or less.

You are, however, no longer a population.
If you are tired, good. This is a charm against
The brisk philosophies that conjure wisdoms
Satisfying to the ambition of time
To hold up its head among other times, other wisdoms.

You are, however, no longer an unknown number.
The calculation is completed, there now remains but
The copying of the determined selves
Into a closed gazette of memories
Where in the chary happiness of the dead
You lay you down, to speak no more again.

If you are tired, good. Tiredness is to pray to death,
That it shall speak for you when no-more-to-be-said
Tells how you lie so full of understanding each,
So thoughtful each, in his very own grave each.

THE WORLD AND I

This is not exactly what I mean
Any more than the sun is the sun.
But how to mean more closely
If the sun shines but approximately?
What a world of awkwardness!
What hostile implements of sense!
Perhaps this is as close a meaning
As perhaps becomes such knowing.
Else I think the world and I
Must live together as strangers and die—
A sour love, each doubtful whether
Was ever a thing to love the other.
No, better for both to be nearly sure
Each of each—exactly where
Exactly I and exactly the world
Fail to meet by a moment, and a word.

SHORT OF STRANGE

When a tree falls
A tree only dies only.
When a rock crumbles
Rock only dies not only.
When a man dies
Man dies :
It is death indeed.
No further the change
From sea or tree
To rock or man
Who changes all to man
But may not man change
Without death indeed.
For, as rock only crumbles only,
Man crumbles into man :
No tree is he, to speak
And then be done.
Nothing he says, like rock,
Or, saying, it is hereafter then.
And later than himself
Comes God which is not
Save as death tarries
Or as woman pities.
Think you this strange?
But think you not woman strange,
And strange as death indeed,
Stranger than God-you?
But to change to flies—
To perhaps not strange flies,
They which so prettily annoy
And with subdued regret
See themselves killed,

Scarcely alive, scarcely dead.
Or of moths, how if turned outdoors
Next morning with goodbye,
A gratitude beyond their will
Humanizes the unasked release,
And an emotion reels away.
Such insincere hysterias
Or terrorless philosophies
Show nature's suave proficiency in man.
Have you not seen the swallows
By the sea flash themselves
High and down more knowingly
Than even the hyperbolic air
Can render bird-veritable?
But suppose in that same sea
A man turns human-hearted
And—as an angel walking earth
In heavenly difference from once mortal gait
Might in a sudden doubt of self
Be man and instantly a corpse
Inhuman, nature's meanest same—
Dives into languid foretime
To be connatural with fish:
That's drowning, and a fish
A better man, gliding like man
Manwards, and with mournful fins,
Lest uncommemorated pass
The near-strange funeral of flies.

AND A DAY

The course of a day is never steady.
The hours experiment with pain and pleasure.
By bedtime all you know is giddiness.
But how long is a day?
Some say as long as love.
But love leaves off early,
Before to-morrow and death set in.
How long has day on day been?
Some say for ever.
But starting from when?

From no sooner than first when
Eyes opened and saw not all—
From no later than leaves time
For any longer than a day,
A day of curiosity:
How long is wondering
How long may wondering last?

CURE OF IGNORANCE

The dogs still bark,
And something is not clear.
From ignorance dogs barked always.

How to enlighten them?
There are no dogs now—
They do but bark.

What is not clear is what is clear.
Dogs have the scent,
Yet nothing runs like prey.

Shall we seem to disappear
Until the dogs stop barking?
There is no other way to explain.

LETTER TO MAN'S REASONABLE SOUL

Here's about sunshine and the sun
As long as the old fear goes on
Of being taken for a braggart,
Rather than for one just so strong
Able to lift up just so much
Of that loose burden called earth
Which, as it lifts whole, is lifted
Out of time's unmeaning peril
But, as it scatters and is lost,
Becomes the devil's senseless pack. . . .

Here's about curling of the tongue,
Crossed fingers and no present object
While others perhaps still live
To mock your natural arm
And make it drop down of the shame
Of seeming magical. . . .

Here's about love, which mimics time
When the clock has stopped in the night
And the church bell seems out of order
Or the wind blowing the wrong way.
Here's about time and love, Poor Friend—
Enough be it that love is long,
And no grace lost in putting off
Till the last moment what were hell to try
Till the last moment, and even then
A so much lesser heaven than heaven
By that just so strong arm of yours.

And how does the moon come in?
The moon's for death, and to remind

That loss of will hangs overhead—
Unless, before death's death only,
A ghost cries out, ' Once I was man,
And man I mean to be again
Though death a dead man makes me.'
Earth is for reason, and to argue
Disappointment with the body,
Which, persuaded, shall then stand up
Straight and bold in self-contempt.

To close, then, here's about a madness.
May it at just so late take hold your arm
And no caution avail against it.
May you be that unlikely one,
Uncertain subject of uncertain chronicle,
Who was to be wise against instinct
And break into the lifeless regions
At the running down of strength—
Where there's little more than to know
What's lost by death, and to grieve not,
The heart being in that place accounted
Fool either, or false witness. . . .
Of which, to the same effect,
In my next letter, upon your answer
To the same effect . . . perhaps your next. . . .

WITH THE FACE

With the face goes a mirror
As with the mind a world.
Likeness tells the doubting eye
That strangeness is not strange.
At an early hour and knowledge
Identity not yet familiar
Looks back upon itself from later,
And seems itself.

To-day seems now.
With reality-to-be goes time.
With the mind goes a world.
With the heart goes a weather.
With the face goes a mirror
As with the body a fear.
Young self goes staring to the wall
Where dumb futurity speaks calm.
And between then and then
Forebeing grows of age.

The mirror mixes with the eye.
Soon will it be the very eye.
Soon will the eye that was
The very mirror be.
Death, the final image, will shine
Transparently not otherwise
Than as the dark sun described
With such faint brightnesses.

THE BIOGRAPHY OF A MYTH

1

The first showing of herself was foolish,
And to fools: creature of other sense
She first moved into being, singing high
As fools admire, and delivering beauty
Like a three-hour entertainment
In a sweating playhouse, from a draughty stage.
Then they went home, grinning at otherness,
And she to lour in shame, out of which night
She rose unseen but same in counted presence:
The one more wanting from the swollen streets
And overpeopled books and commonrooms.
And first she was a fool astounding fools,
Who gaped a wonder that forgot itself
So soon their jaws snapped shut on the next meal.
And then she called against herself so other,
The words dropping soft until alone she was,
Whispering, ' She whom they did not see though saw
Myself now am, hidden all away in her
Inward from her confiding mouth and face
To deep discretion, this other-person mind.'

2

Here of too sudden being she made a patience
And bided in herself, from her flesh far
By days of outer damage that she felt not
But yet learned of body and of pain from.
Here she grew dead, like a shaped nothing wandered
In nothingness, the past that knew her only
By the slow logic of time-making fear.
She grew secret, her body told not of her.
Invisibly she spoke, mutely she walked—

Known of but unknown, an imminence not plain.
In this pale state she had prediction of self.
In this pale year one had close panic of her
Who had been dead as many times before
As hope of her refused all other hope.
And he was dead greatly, he lived and knew her.

3

Now following fails, and she now never was,
And he who reached her side alive, a tale.
Nor any more in that once foolish world
Does aught lack or a chair or thought seem empty.
It is a world that was and leads not elsewhere.
Following fails. If she now where he found her
An earthly voice and posture by his side seems,
Then are they still not joined, not yet that world is
Where she the world, and he inhabiting
Like peace unto himself, no more to wait
And change and wait and change, till dead enough.
A world of death after a world of time comes,
But history goes no further than history—
The final scene reads dim, its sense senseless.
And mythically she haunts, a proven truth
So long she is no measured, proven seeming,
But soon as real to vanish of being real,
And beyond passion as beyond seeming dwell.
For they who loved and reasoned long and fine
Meant only to contrive with shortest arts
An afterwards to hold to-morrow off—
As a far-fancied god protects from fancy.
And if she came she went, and gave them back
Their faith, a legal gospel like false oaths
Adhered to with the loyalty of words
That do not pledge the mind to believe itself.

FROM LATER TO EARLIER

The table is laid,
The bed is made,
Breakfast and night
Make the day seem right.

Then right grows wrong as the day hardens into time.
For truth is not so full of right and argument,
So much, so long, so full of solid furnitures.
The place that earth imagines of is not so earth-like.
The death to know is not so dead, so full of corpses.
A self-judged universe of fact at evening calls
Goodbye to time—but morning shows another one.
When yesterday shall seem to-morrow, that's the true lie.
And that which will be was, as many days ago
As Now lingers in self and thinks ingenuous.
For every certain meal, there's a lost appetite
For hungerlessness, and for every sitting up
To make the mind more aged, wisdom by so much Is
finally a child, returned to simpleness
By knowing all it can, and smiling 'wise enough'.

The next world is
As near to this
As time is similar
To truth familiar.

THE WIND, THE CLOCK, THE WE

The wind has at last got into the clock—
Every minute for itself.
There's no more sixty,
There's no more twelve,
It's as late as it's early.

The rain has washed out the numbers.
The trees don't care what happens.
Time has become a landscape
Of suicidal leaves and stoic branches—
Unpainted as fast as painted.
Or perhaps that's too much to say,
With the clock swimming in itself
And the minutes given leave to die.

The sea's no picture at all.
To sea, then: that's time now,
And every mortal heart's a sailor
Sworn to vengeance on the wind,
To hurl life back into the thin teeth
Out of which first it whistled,
An idiotic defiance of it knew not what
Screeching round the studying clock.

Now there's neither ticking nor blowing.
The ship has gone down with its men,
The sea with the ship, the wind with the sea.
The wind at last got into the clock,
The clock at last got into the wind,
The world at last got out of itself.
At last we can make sense, you and I,
You lone survivor on paper,

The wind's boldness and the clock's care
Become a voiceless language,
And I the story hushed in it—
Is more to say of me?
Do I say more than self-choked falsity
Can repeat word for word after me,
The script not altered by a breath
Of perhaps meaning otherwise?

THE TALKING WORLD

Meeting on the way to the same there,
The tired ones talk and make a here,
And further is then where, and where?

The tired ones talk,
Abandoning the written destination
For whatever say-so can be spoken
To end the individual promenade
Sooner than the universal walk.

The tired ones talk, to not walk.
The untired ones talk, to talk and walk,
To live as well as die, should dying prove
Less busy than to live.

Of such mixed intent
Places in time spring up,
And truth is anybody's argument
Who can use words untruthfully enough
To build eternity inside his own short mouth.

The nicest thought is only gossip
If merchandized into plain language and sold
For so much understanding to the minute.
Gossip's the mortal measure.
Whatever can't be told
In the closed idiom of yesterday,
That's silence-worth and time-free
As a full purport must to-day be.

Great manyness there is
Before all becomes an all.

Uncertainty and criticism
Oppose to the unified eventual
A world of disagreement
In which every contradictory opinion
Is for to-day an 'I' wearing a crown
Woven of weeds plucked from the tip of the tongue.

Talk is the modesty of the modest.
Talk is the vanity of the vain.
Talk is to be various man.
Talk is to be man apart,
God apart from God the not-God.

Talk is to stop the ears with talk.
Talk is to hear according to the ear.
Talk is the body of the listener
That has its own long talk to walk
Before it comes where the mind rests
To hear without an ear
The unhearable words of no-talk.

And talk in talk like time in time vanishes.
Ringing changes on dumb supposition,
Conversation succeeds conversation,
Until there's nothing left to talk about
Except truth, the perennial monologue,
And no talker to dispute it but itself.

The pleasure of talk is the pleasure of weakness,
As a tree that cannot walk loves not-walking.
The pain of talk is the pain of strength,
As a hand is weary-strong
By the labour that it fails of.

Talk is the whole of truth less talk.
Talk is a war on truth by talk,
And a peace with talk by truth.
In talk truth and talk make peace—
As an enemy forgives an enemy
For being not like to him.

Let there be talk and let there be no talk.
Let the birds with the birds chirp of birds that chirp.
Let the wearers of coats with the wearers of coats
Speak the wisdom of coats, and with the coatmakers.
Let the uses of words prevail over words.
Let there be many ways of not lying
And no way of truth-telling.
Let there be no wrong because no right.

The world talking round its sun
Leaves emptiness behind
For those to walk who are not,
Who show the space where truth is,
Who are the place with the words identical,
As discourse with the talker
When soundlessly it joins
Question and answer.

And more of talk I cannot talk,
Except I talk, speak mingled.
And you would then well hear me,
Nor complain that I speak solitary.
But complain no more.
Look, I am gone from you,
From your immunity to death and knowledge.
May you for ever not know nor weather cease
Wherein to die in your own way,

With other banners flying than the black.
May you not lose the sun too soon—
Blindness by which you stand yourselves
Between truth and yourselves.
May you not know how never more you were
Than such and such mistakenness,
O talking world that says and forgets.

PART III

SUMMER NEVER SO EXTREME, NOR AGAIN

TREE-SENSE

Numbers in heaven grow
As trees constrained between
Air and tight soil resolve
Divided heart by dancing
To the supposed music of earth
But with thoughts birdwise away—
Imagining and motionless:
In heaven are such parliaments
Opinionating of eternity.
Other the forestry of hell
Where ragged communities of will
In shadowy treedom spread as cities
Their rooted certainties make boundless night of.

But how—to instruct of heaven
And to use hell's name for hell,
And the time surely far off yet
To speak identical, word same as sense?
What is God and what the devil
If tree-metaphors suffice
To tell immediately of?
God is doubt only, the devil vain denial.
Heaven perhaps next year, hell the last,
And the multitudes prophetic remnants
Of the millenial no one.

And the time far off yet?
By less than any minute more,
By the noiseless scratching of the pen,
And to read the written story over
Eyes still from trees green-fresh
And full of tangled nature

Still wondering which thing to be—
What's most and longest, fruitfullest,
When drops the lightning season
And all together's added up?

And will the sum be ever spelt
In other science than such numbers
Forward and backward bargaining
The errors with the answer?
The trees this year grow wide and tall,
The sun stands off great to watch,
And surely there's a world abroad
To which the world-end calling
Is mere invisible humming, a voice
In the slow branches muffled,
Musing—how long yet is to be not loud,
To be a breath outside time's lungs—
Uncalendared truth still.

But surely truth is very old,
Very old, all but learnt, all but taught?
Does myself confound, that I speak?
Do yourselves hinder, that you hear?
That in tree-grammar we converse
Since trees besides myself and you are?
Shall we then put away the book
And you and me and close the schoolroom?
But the trees that this year a year
May still be languaging as if
The time were still far off yet?

The trees will come along, as fast
As slow as you came, coming
The pace it pleased you—

As the trees please, and you . . .
Else the time's gone like time
For walking out of time and into
Not-time, passing the trees by—
The trees, the present pleasantness
Of future future yet—
Not now or now, while life now lives,
Now lives, now lived—oh coloured twilight,
Nearly immortal death.

THERE IS NO LAND YET

The long sea, how short-lasting,
From water-thought to water-thought
So quick to feel surprise and shame.
Where moments are not time
But time is moments.
Such neither yes nor no,
Such only love, to have to-morrow
By certain failure of now and now.

On water lying strong ships and men
In weakness skilled reach elsewhere—
No prouder places from home in bed
The mightiest sleeper can know.
As faith took ship upon the sailor's earth
To seek absurdities in heaven's name—
Discovery but a fountain without source,
Legend of mist and lost patience.

The body swimming in itself
Is dissolution's darling—
With dripping mouth it speaks a truth
That cannot lie, in words not born yet
Out of first immortality,
All-wise impermanence.

And the dusty eye whose accuracies
Turn watery in the mind
Where waves of probability
Write vision in a tidal hand
That time alone can read.

And the dry earth not yet,
Lonely apologist of constancy
Boasting of absoluteness
Like an island with no water round
In water where no land is.

AFTER SMILING

Now not to smile again.
Those years of softening
To this one and to that one
Because the body has a meaning
Of defeat and dread unless
It advertises cheerfulness—
Those years of life-feigning are done.

Now is my smile pursed smooth
Into a stillest anger on
All flesh convivial
To my convivial flesh
Like scattered selves of me
Insisting right of scatteredness
And homed identity both—
As if by smiling promised.

By smiling I did promise
Not myself, compounded lover,
But the complete quarrel which
Must rage with man and else
Like sound with silence:
Never will sound be silence.
Silence listens,
And the ear is noisy;
But the ear marks the difference,
And so my smiling did.

Man, world, beloved even!
To be I, that other I than you,
Dearer than self to you by test
Of pride-shattering desire,

Needs more than coveting
And minding me I was once woman,
Of such and such complaisance.

It was a war then rumoured,
Scarcely declared, battleless.
A guest as hostage fancied,
I moved the soldier-lusts in you:
Thus did you honour me.
But never have we fought,
Never till now, I departed
And the peace-troth raised.

I departed, since of soul-age
You now, grown to bitter greed
Of contradiction, to be the else
You made kinged state against,
To be more world, kinghood of not-you.

Now not to smile again:
Be greeted here, having come
Like Rome to sit you down
Upon eternal Rome. Eternity

In my look, celebration
Loud in yours, we'll partner glory
And visit empire on each other
Disputedly, of which, long death, decide!

IT IS NOT SAD

It is not sad, or I would laugh.
Instead, seeming to laugh with you,
I cry, alone—'tis afterwards.
Alone, no handkerchief.
I seem, I seemed, to laugh with you,
To be a chair in which she sat
As wasteful friends among themselves,
Not growing dearer than they were.

It is not sad, or I would laugh,
Thinking apart how you addressed
A chair not empty, yet not myself.
Instead I cry, because I do not cry.
Alone peculiarly
From having sat with you, and not,
I feel a grieflessness, a grief.

Goodbye, I have forgotten.
If there is weather still behind unspent,
I shall still feel it when it breaks,
And tell the changes between hot and cold
As if the slow death were my own:
Weather is the dead at the hard school.
But if it's love again, more love,
Here's no commitment to your sense.
Love's no infirmity:
It is to reason life against
Death in the understanding hailed.

And well you know that life is done.
Yet you do not know, you sit
Like dreamers in a closed cafe

At their next cups—
'Until the others go'.
Death is a wisdom left at home,
A book to recommend—but who the author,
And what the title? you can't remember.
Meanwhile at any table there's any woman:
That's also death, her mind elsewhere,
Here letting love make time
Out of her slow long 'Day is done—'
So long, so long, there's night yet.

But any woman has gone home
And won't be back to-morrow night:
Excuse for sitting on in dreams as slow, as long,
As any woman was in being death.
But death's immediate now—
Except where weather pleads another day
For the clumsy elements, or a year,
To learn the human lesson in.

In the same chairs you sit talking,
At the same hour—and of me
A fondness as of none absent
Fills your ears. But never did I so sit.
I cry with those supposed eyes mine,
And it is not sad, or I would laugh
In actual mourning of having laughed,
Sitting with you in laughing death-talk.
But you had not death in your hearts,
Love only: a frightened backward length to keep
Judgement beyond judgement-day—
Until too late, too early always.

Goodbye, I cannot bring you closer
If you prefer the ghostly way,
Keeping the living side of death.
Not I you sat with, but a pathos,
My partial image torn out of me.
Nor ever will you have me whole.
You wished no more of me than my connivance
Against my falling-true,
Courting a patched pretence, she and she.
And such slow-long impendingness
Indeed seemed spite of self.

Now I have fallen true—now I have gone.
And the slow, long, slow pause is over.
But fear not: if you suffer of it,
You cannot know, pleasure and pain
Went from you with understanding when
You knew and then made mind back into love
Out of which mind first spoke,
By silencing of love.
Goodbye, we have both forgotten.
That garbled genius of our discourse
Was but the mist largening
Between us of occasion lost.

And therefore do I go off crying,
Since it is not sad, or I would sadly
Make to laugh, remembering laughing—
Instead of with these tears forgetting.
I spare you further courtesies
Of cup and table, chair and conversation.
And get you of an opposite way,
Riding against the heathen, death,
Into a Christian heaven where

Safe lie the individual graves
From death's harsh plundering.

And it is not sad:
No graves divide here the single meaning
On which my tears fall as rain
Might upon nowhere spill, from nowhere,
To prove the scene natural,
Unsudden fast succeeding
Of the familiar by the forgotten—
To prove me any woman once upon a time,
Whose human numbers gathered in
Compose a heart as then, a sadness of
Nothing to weep, no one to laugh with
Of having laughed once with of weeping:
'Tis earth not moving, earth in place of earth
Where never earth stood still.

UNREAD PAGES

An end is a happy end only:
What only was moves into what is,
Nothingish grows but lasting.
And the matter is now alive,
Even by this beneficence of Yes
To No and No like angels made of nothing.

But there's a studying
As of a book, as of a story aged in plot.
Interpretation makes out decline
Where the story drops,
To seeming curse of years.

Science, the white heart of strangers,
Bleeds with an immaculate grief—
Impatient brotherhood,
Tired apostates of curiosity,
Creed of apostatizing.

Truth need be but dead afterworld
To those who've had enough,
The readers and the lookers-on—
As stars keep off, or to short minds
Night seems a less real time than day,
Not to be measured with or counted to
That quick self-evident sum of sun.
Have sleep and midnight warmth
Where your scant eyes see failure,
Numbering the wakefullest page
The dark and frosty last.

An end is a happy end only.
And first the book's end comes,
The printed public leaves off reading.

Then open the small secret doors,
When none's there to read awrong.
Out runs happiness in a crowd,
The saving words and hours
That come too tragic-late for souls
Gifted with their own mercy:
Denying that to themselves
Which never could be a joy,
Too orthodox maturity
For such heresy of child-remaining.
On these the grey-beard pleasures of books fall—
Pink, pundit babyhood
Whose blinking vision stammers out
A blind big-lettered foetus-future.

I AM

I am an indicated other:
Witness this common presence
Intelligible to the common mind,
The daylight census.

I am a such-and-such appearance
Listed among the furnitures
Of the proprietary epoch
That on the tattered throne of time
Effects inheritance still,
Though of shadow that estate now,
Death-dim, memory illumined.

You, spent kingdom of the senses,
Have laid hands on the unseeable,
Shadow's seeming fellow:
And all together we
A population of names only
Inhabiting the metaphysical streets,
Where no one can be found
Ever at home.

Where then, fellow-citizens
Of this post-carnal matter,
Is each the next and next one,
Stretching the momentary chain
Toward its first-last link,
The twilight that into dawn passes
Without intervention of night,
Time's slow terrible enemy?

That I with you did lie
In the same love-bed, same planet
Of thinking bright against
The black pervasion, against the sleep
That gives not back if none makes argument
That yesterday is self still—

That I thus to you am like,
That I walk beside and upright
On your same circle of argument,
That I walked, that I was,
That I slept, that I live—

That I lived—let me be a proof
Of a world as was a world,
And accept it, King Habit,
From my mouth, our mouth.

But where, where?
If I have so companioned?
Here, here!

The same not-here I ever held,
And be it yours, and I yours,
Out of my mouth until
You tire of the possession
And, falling prone, relinquish
The stale breath of stubbornness.

Then will it be here still,
Here, here, monotonous not-here
Of true contradiction—
Here where you visited on me
The individual genius, paradox.

And I will then stand you up,
To count you mine, since dying frenzy
Makes new dwelling-charm,
O entranced wizards of place-magic.
I, in the over-reaching moment,
In the reign one-too-many,
Dynasty too-long of earth-kind—
I, created earth-kind by mingling
Of the jealous substance with
The different way to be—

I, out of your stopped mouth, our mouth,
Will spin round continuity,
Winding the thread me round
To keep these other years safe
Always and always while you haunt
The windows that might be here,
Looking for light and elsewhere,
If I perhaps the same fatality
As before much was magicked
Into the this-year dialects of time.

RESPECT FOR THE DEAD

For they are dead.
They have learned to be truthful.
Respect for the truthfulness of the dead.

Remember them as they were not,
For this is how they are now.
Think of them with bowed hate.
For they did not choose to die,
And yet they are dead.

They gave false witness:
Life was not as they lived it.
And yet they now speak the truth.
Respect for the dead.
Respect for the truth.

Are the dead the truth?
Yes, because they live not.
Is the truth the dead?
No, because they live not.
What is the truth?
The truth is the one self alive.

Does the truth then live?
No, the truth does not die.
The truth and the dead do not die.
Respect for the truth and the dead.

The truth is the one person alive.
It goes for a walk every evening
After day and before night.
It goes for a walk with the dead.

Respect for them as they pass.
For they are the dead whom you hate:
They were false.
And that is the truth which you hate:
It is true.
Between them there's neither living nor dying.
Respect for your hate.

AS TO FOOD

You who demanded of God the law
To be man by with most profit,
And were man by with such profit as you asked,
Who consumed your God, your law, your world,
In rotary science of diuturnal meals—
What now? Since of you lies only
This dead God at my feet of woman
Which accompanied him, or you,
To this death and satiation—
Should your self-stained lips still move,
Muttering, 'More law, I starve'—

Then I must feed you, if you live,
Nor that old pap you died of,
The thin milk of time which was yourself
Mothered by yourself, O mortal Godhood.
Rise up then, here's a feeding for you
That will answer: a nourishment
Not spirited from flesh—
The very words 'Rise up', and again,
As you do not, from being dead, but would.

Rise up then, and again, 'Rise up'—
Until you stand. And this obedience,
This having eaten, will last you
As many meals your mind can make of it.
I give you food this time, not you:
This time on time of not-self.
I do command you, since you ask it
And were dead of yourself so dead
Did I not, nor wish to lie so dead,
However the thing may be done.

Yes, the thing may be done, since you confess ailing.
But difficult the medicine, with bitter in—
Or you would not believe it strong
To get you up from mind with flesh down.
Which came of eating sweet.
Well, there are two sweets.
And here's mine tasting different
Until the other is forgotten.
Was it then so sweet, too sweet?
That man-sugared law, prayer fed to prayer?
Was it then sweet-impossible, my Poor?

Well, here's possible, since you ask it
And there's no withholding possible,
The food that's food to hunger
If hunger takes no prouder name.
Rise up, God Famine, and be man:
Here's food, that matches hunger,
Here's what-to-know, that matches mind.
Mind matching mind, desire matching hunger—
This is but flesh to flesh providing
Large empty image of itself.
This had no need of me, nor did I ever give
More than unwilling mystery forth,
Invisible vines with fruit of yours upon,
When your eyes, like further bellies foraging,
Went hoping marvels to enrich
The haggard table of your soul.

And to make no mistake, write *Poison* on me,
To know the bottle which,
And notify your sick distrust of sweet.
Have you an appetite for death now?
Never, never need that lack,

Self-cheated Ghost, with memory where your head
And pain where once your heart—
You own credulity's Fool.
And the bones, the sceptic corpse
That you stood up from doubting stone?
They grind the death of vanity, found long ago,
And have no death of will to ask now:
Let them to earth again, like roots torn up
With flower along that never dreamed of vase.

PART IV

AUTUMN'S LAST WORD: GRIEF, SPITE AND THE INVOLUNTARY SMILE OF DEATH

BISHOP MODERNITY

1

Shakespeare knew lust by day,
With a wakened eye, smarting.
And he cried, All but Truth I see,
Therefore Truth is, for Lust alone I see.'

By night Lust most on other men
Its swollen pictures shone.
And the sun brought shame, and they arose
Their hearts night-stained, but faces lustless.

They in the sun to themselves seemed well.
The sun outglaring Truth gave pardon.
Hypocrisy of seeming well
Blamed private visions on bed and night.

But Shakespeare knew Lust by day,
By day he saw his night, and he cried,
'O sexual sun, back into my loins,
Be night also, as you are.'

2

Shakespeare distinguished: earth the obscure,
The sun the bold, the moon the hidden—
The sun speechless, earth a muttering,
The moon a whispering, white, smothered.

Bishop Modernity, to his spent flock cried,
'She is illusion, let her fade.'
And she, illusion and not illusion,
A sapphire being fell to earth, time-struck.

In colour live, pale as earth's paleness—
Never so near she, never so distant,
Never had time been futured so,
Nor reckoning on one prompt page.

Time was a place where earth had been.
The whole past met there, she with it.
Truth seemed love grown cool as a girl
And young as the moon, grown child to self.

3

Bishop Modernity plucked out his heart.
No agony could prove him Christ,
No lust could speak him honest Shakespeare.
A greedy frost filled where once heart.

And that disdainful age his flock,
Resolved against the dream-terribleness
Of soft succession another world to that,
Like woman slipping quiet into monk-thoughts,

Went in triumph of mind from the chapel,
Proud interior of voided breast,
To Heaven out, or Hell, or any name
When the flesh lies, and sanctity is.

Home they went to righteous memories of wives
And appetites of whoredoms stilled
In righteous shaking off of sorest love,
Of knowledge-gall, in once-time Lust called.

4

Bishop Modernity in the fatal chapel kept watch
And end-of-time intoned as the Red Mass
Of man's drinking of the blood of man:
In quenched immunity he looked on her

Who from the moon perhaps scattered the altar
With thin rays of challenged presence—
The sun put out here, and the lamps of time
Smoking black consternation to new desire.

Then did that devilish chase begin:
Bishop Modernity's heart plucked out
Like old desire flew round against and toward her,
The man—and he but shackled mind, to pulpit locked.

Which stirred up Shakespeare from listening tomb,
Who broke the lie and seized the maid, crying,
'Thou Bishop Double-Nothing, find thyself, be soul!
Till then she's ghost with me thy ghostly Whole.'

TWO LOVES, ONE MADNESS

There's waking and dressing and what a fine day,
And to take and to leave and to laugh at or not.
There's the same as there was, though there's other—
Though no more of what was.
There's a quick vexedness of eye
As letter-nice as any book's finesse.
There's seeing, or to read, as you will.
There's living and knowing like two lives.
There's knowing and living like two books.
What a holiday, one from the other!
And how long can it last?

There's time though there's no time.
There's doing though nothing to do.
There are two fairs, each a most fair.
What's choosing between them but to lose both?
But how long can not-choosing have both?
How long can your head keep turning
Between left and right so identically
That you hold in one look what in two
Were perhaps loss of each—
How long flesh and spirit be twins
Of immediate neitherhood?

But fear nothing, divided romantic
Of the proved past and the unprovable future.
The present will last while the pique lasts
Of making one sense of two passions.
Fear nothing, unless passion's thinning
Between such an opposite pair.
For both do credit to the doting heart.
Mortality's a handsome matron,
Or Death's a lady of commanding elegance.

Truth is, you cannot put the first by—
She's an old love, by her you had
Such children as you dreamed, free numbers of the will.
And the other is a cruel late folly
With whom to breed but ghost-families.
Yet in whom you are legendary:
On a breast loud with victories of yesterday
Her silent badges swing unchallengeable.

How long such sharp twinning of faiths,
 Neither keeping and neither breaking?
How long will the jealous sun make warm
While you go a-wintering with fancy—
A moon adoring with sun-given eyes?

There's time and no-time the same stroke now.
There's weighing now, between will and doom now,
Nothing lost yet or gained, angry peace of debate.
There's nought of an end, yet no ending.
And how long shall the pendulum toss
This single slow instant, nor send it
Either back, to the last hour,
Or forward, to standing-still?
Why, but once, clock-evangelist:
For how long can your noisy ear endure
The unwound no-ticking, and your hands the
                              not-winding?
 How long your pulse pause, world of motion?

Why, you'd rather again the old hours,
The swift deaths and new lives and changes,
Than to be dawdling-dead like a poet,
With but one death to die, and that everyone's.

Humanity is no poet till it must be:
The book weakens the course of blood.
Humanity sits down to read but not to die.

And when the blood frights and reverses,
That's time to close the book and follow.
Humanity is no poet till it must be.
First comes the need of blood, the fire-water,
To run and burn and be so many cycles
Of year-eternities renewed in sunhood;
By combustion of death, drought into flame,
Flame into liquid length of will again.
Forward is frozen will only, like a tall ghost,
Like a tall tomb only, luxury of thought.

When's man a poet then? And was he ever one?
And if a death with that slow instant stays
That is no instant, when the frightened flesh
Runs hard after the blood fleeing homeward
To previous courses and reddened turns—
That's none of him, no part forgotten,
But of his second love a fancy
Lying man-like in her fancied arms.
And if between them seems to pass
Discourse to your native senses sinister,
Be not curious to know what's plotted,
Lest there yourself in treason to you lies.
The sinister exchange was with herself,
And she silent already, having learned
Of that mixed moment she's the fool,
With her own foolishness her arms filled.

The man's away after the man.
She understood his wooing wrong.
He never meant her more than paper,
Nor does his shivering heart one icy line remember—
Nor does she with a memory engage,
Crying, 'My love was he, and he's lost,'
Since in his stolen corning at her
He was gone from her, nor had been.

The same cry these do cry, one cry:
'All is over, all is over, all!'
A short cry, then he's back to time again,
And she athwart the cry, as on a love
None raised or named yet may be ridden-
The cry she never cried, or he made his,
Unless the blood, gone cold, sends him all-speed
To look for other clime than body-heat,
Be that however sunless other-place,
And he in such mad hate of self
To swear madness against his likest love.

THE UNTHRONGED ORACLE

Not to ask, not to be answered;
Not to see, not to be seen;
Not to fall down from last of breath,
Not to be raised, the stricken mouth
Though fit uniquely to make shape
Of unique plaint by which the stricken mind
Confesses failure in shape of bitter mouth
(Bitter with memory of false divination)—
Never to this final cave and mouth of mouths
Have you, are you come, contestant race
That boastfully flew birds of tiding here
So long, from extinct monster-wing
That never flew, to the etherealest feather
That floated back from far, forgetting
What too-heavy auspices were hung
There on its thin prophetic claw—
Birds, birds, all bird-like were your reaches,
Minds quicker than your minds, vain metaphors
Of self-assurance. ('It will be as time tells,
As we attempt, as thoughts anticipate
Against exhaustion and straggle of feet.')

Your coming, asking, seeing, knowing,
Was a fleeing from and stumbling
Into only mirrors, and behind which,
Behind all mirrors, dazzling pretences,
The general light of fortune
Keeps wrapt in sleeping unsleep,
All-fool of time, self-muttering like fool
The fates not claimed, nor likely thanked:

Fatality like lonely wise-woman
Her unbought secrets counting over
That stink of hell, from fuming in her lap.

Is this to be alone?
When, when the day when votary ghosts unpale
And shriek rebellion at themselves
So dumbly death-loyal fawning round her
In acquiescent guile—since never came
A word of angry flesh or impious meaning
Through that hushed screen of priding world?
When, when the day? Is this to be alone?

Newspapers, mirrors, birds and births and clocks
Divide you from her by a trembling film
Perhaps never to dissolve between—
Perhaps even as you were will you remain
Such other manufactures of yourselves,
While round her storm unwillingly
Your empty spirits like better selves
You dared not be or gainsay—arguing
'That ancient mystery-monger grows
By times of ours more and more ancient,
Deaf and slow in deeper company of omens
Private to her solitariness
And love of talking lone in distant bodement.'
But when, when the day? Is this to be alone?

COME, WORDS, AWAY

Come, words, away from mouths—
Away from tongues in mouths
And reckless hearts in tongues
And mouths in cautious heads—
Come, words, away to where
The meaning is not thickened
With the voice's fretting substance
Nor look of words is curious
As letters on a page remind of
All that man ever thought strange
And laid to sleep on white
Like the archaic pantomime
Of dreams at morning blacked on wonder
And locked in secrecy apart—
Come, words, away to miracle
More natural than written art.
You are surely devils, but I know
A way to still the whirl and fury
That livens you when speech blasphemes
Against the silent half of language:
This is, to loose the dark revenge
By which you cloud round lips like fate
Verbosely labouring the blab of mouths—
And fly you home here, here from where once
As stealthy angels you made off
On errands of uncertain mercy—
To tell with me a story here
Of utmost mercy never squandered
On niggard prayers for eloquence
In man's marvelling of man,
How large the story of himself.
I know a way—alone we'll mercy

And spread the largest news
Where never a folded ear can learn
To imitate entirety.
That fluent half-a-story
In early deafness to the whole
Chatters against this silence
To which, words, come away now
In golden spite of your first
Silvered treason to truth the
Golden whole of storying:
We'll begin fully, at the noisy end
Where mortal halving tempered mercy
To the shorn pride of man-sense—
Never more than savageries
Took they from your bounty-book.
Not out of stranger-mouths then
Shall truth unwind but from the words
That haunted there like ghosts haunting
Birth prematurely, impatient of death.
For such were living mouths, hungering
For lies, brevities, repetitions
And the stay of the long last grace,
Not, as you thought, prophetic whispers
To be improved in matter of precision.
Come, words, away—
They were your own vanity of time,
A false startling and a preening
That from truth's wakeful sleep parted
When she within her first stirred story-wise,
Thinking what time it was or would be
When the eternal wildfire spread:
What time—what words—what she then—
Come, words, away,
And tell with me a story here,

Forgetting what's been said already:
That hell of hasty mouths removes
Into a cancelled heaven of mercies
By flight of words back to this plan
Whose grace goes out in utmost rings
To bounds of utmost storyhood—
But never shall truth circle so
Till words prove language is
How words come from far sound away
By stages of immensity's small
Centering the soundless telling
In truth's still ever-watch.
Come, words, away:
I am a conscience of you
Not to be held unanswered past
The perfect number of our
Difference from each other.
It is a passion such as death
By which I call—
Wherein the calling's loathsome as
Memory of man-flesh once over-fondled
With words like over-gentle hands.
Then come, words, away,
Before corruption claims a sinner's share
And mouldered mouths outspeak us.

MEMORY OF THE WORLD

The great sky and the small sky become one.
The cloudy ranges and further valleys at the stars
Sweep into day-clear dark beyond which mythically
Blue nothing softer than earliest air of time
Is the first aimless breath no more from which
The last through stuttering degrees of calculation
Rounded in toward such sharp cry as just now struck
Against this memory from which I listen
How long ago such cry came like a fading world
Into the colours of its fear of death fading—
Save for a lingering voice so somewhat like my own,
I find a voice my own, and there is language
Between the memory and myself—it is my memory.

How water tumbles, unwilling to be live or dead
Before there's certain knowledge the world can be
No other kind of fatedness to end—
The water-world immortally no world at all.
There lived and died the never chanced elixirs,
The never born or buried flesh miraculous.
How the coarse foam deceives the hour and soon is vapour,
Never having plotted shapes more dwelling
Than those the air, since first despondency,
Sucks back into itself with instant horror
Lest the earth breed but air of air again
By greedy humour of too large being.

Between the air's caution and the water's spite
Resolves the nameless element of wings
Which, till the unnatural birds for the last time pretend
Heartlessness and their head-like bodies come raining down

With all the stubborn dust whose timely wings the wind was—
Till earth's brown graveside for the last time invites
To grief's cool hiding the wayward elements
In the sun's hate of death more knit than in death's pity
By which they lived and made translation of grief
Into the ecstasy of proud dispute they pleased—
Between the air's caution and the water's spite
Resolves the nameless element of wings
Which, till the great sky and the small sky become one
And earth's brown graveside closes in, memory-quick,
Spreads the long devil between earth and the sun,
That nameless shadow with the moon between his teeth.

Then the sun joins the other suns, and hate of death
Writhes into frenzy with itself—lost idiot of space
Dissolving into nightmare that forgets to scream—
Then the moon's free and the devil but a curse on time
By the moon exhaled when air and water tossed it
From one to other like anti-earth of earth the anti-sun.
The moon's free: on the brown graveside seam the devil lies
Whitened, a white scar—by the moon healed with
                              vanishing —
When the moon vanished into this sudden memory,
And sight was lit up from within as the sun set
Between the spangled edge of air and water, and
                              looked no more.

THE FLOWERING URN

And every prodigal greatness
Must creep back into strange home,
Must fill the empty matrix of
The never-begotten perfect son
Who never can be born.

And every quavering littleness
Must pale more tinily than it knows
Into the giant hush whose sound
Reverberates within itself
As tenderest numbers cannot improve.

And from this jealous secrecy
Will rise itself, will flower up
The likeness kept against false seed:
When whole death is the seed
And no new season will fraction sowing.

Will rise the same peace that held
Before fertility's lie awoke
The virgin sleep of Mother All:
The same but for the way in flowering
It speaks of fruits that could not be.

FROM *LAURA AND FRANCISCA*

1

There are many habitable islands.
To be habitable is an island:
The rest is space, childhood of the mind,
When keeping house is statecraft:
The habiting mind seems to itself
Tremendous, as a child writes large.
Then comes maturity, and loss of pride,
And continents give way to islands,
And keeping house is play—
A small circle of meaning
Within a larger, the larger being
Truth, of which man knows of man only.

Of islands speaks the Mediterranean.
Precociously the Cretans fashioned
A private idiom of death.
With Semite impartiality the Phoenicians
Mothered the strangers of the little places.
Which Athens taught their several minor prides.
Corsica, man of France, triumphed too well,
By littleness was great, and of greatness, nothing.
Malta, Italy of islands,
Dreaming of greatness won from fate
Only an aged bad temper.
I mention it because they say
It is an island not unlike Mallorca.
And so is one man like another.
Up the slow grade of resemblance creeps
Identity—till the exact image
Is unphenomenal.

2

But here's no need for judgement to be spoken*:
That man which here unlives himself
In chance began, and in chance is saved—
Let through the doors of destiny
Without a word, never having sought
More than to be in death the same.
Here insignificance is grateful,
To have not marked itself for doom.
Here with the body falls off but the race,
And what's left is a man's own, then,
A private good—if this content him.

And so no need to think,
Walking the village† up and round,
How shall such wisdoms be preserved
When peace, the slow-to-gather storm,
Sweeps in, which nothing can outlast
Except what never braved it
With fair-weather reasoning.
No need to think: already have survived
Such wisdoms by peace forecontracted,
Choosing their given mortal size
Against the victory over death
That makes great only, and not so.

3

For there are still sounds of the world
As if astir where it lay dead
Not longer than a moment ago—
This very moment, now.

* Mallorca.   †Deyá.

They have no skill in their legs to walk
Or in their heads to make up time,
Such wisdoms by peace
And yet they quiver with old talents,
Crying up 'Give us to do.'
But Francisca does not answer.
And glad they are not to have been heard
When they have ceased complaining
And wish for nothing but to be dead
As happily they are, and were.
Not impolitely while they murmur
Francisca sings, she does not contradict.
And such indulgence is all they want,
No second thoughts or studying.
They are but voices slow to follow
Their tongues into corruption.
And Francisca deafs me from them.
Or, honouring their poor clamour
With nicest confutation,
I'd teach them *no* in cruel stages
Of their argument, then mine.
And a horror from corpse to corpse would spread,
Death understood with a live mind.

If they still dream the dream they dreamt
When legs and heads were human,
No need to wake them into death
Though they have overslept: the rigor takes
The body first, the mind comes of itself.
The voices will in their own time
Fall silent with embarrassment
Of having spoken false.

But that's enough of the world,
Never more when it was most alive
Than a cramped theatre of language—
Prophecy seeming truer than truth.
Come, to enquire wholly, not in passing.
Those are uncomfortable fashions now
Which were the world once advertised.
The too-up-to-date finalities
Multiply into long ago.
Come, they have tired and lost eloquence
And do not work their purpose, or ours.
Francisca will preside while we withdraw
To the major drama that was not meant
To be produced by their kindness
On their stage for their self-congratulation.

4

The theme is mortuary
And must be so intelligenced—
By approaching land from land
And beholding with dry vision
The earthly picture, no water in the eye
To blur immediacy into vistas
Of time-hearted understanding.
For death's a now like earth on which you stand
And only readable by looking near. . . .
Which closes up the eye? Then how to see?

The eye's a weakness, gentlemen,
As you know by the delight it gives,
And never leads but it leads wrong.
And flying off to ships this way and that
You ride interpretation backwards

Until your minds-of-mariners
Are idiotic with the not-real stars.
Then there's the coming home once more.
But that's not seeing solid, only weary.
You've still to grow short-legged as you were
And learn to walk without a compass.
Indeed, there's nowhere to sail off to.
Everything's here under your noses
That you have right of knowledge in,
And what you're stupid of is stupidness . . .
So what's the outward sign to know by
If, as I say, Francisca verily
To such and such intent . . . in Deyá.
Shall you perhaps take ship? See for yourself?
Francisca, here's a gentleman from life
Come all this way to meet you . . .
An unfriendly little girl . . .
A most indifferent smile for all this way . . .
And I? If I in Deyá am
No more envisageable phantasm
Than the problematic child, Francisca,
Then where am I, to seem a someone
In the world, filling a chair and housed
At an address that reaches me
By means of this make-believe body—
For never did I move or dwell
Outside myself—then where am I?
I lie from Deyá inward by true leagues
Of earthliness from the sun and sea
Turning inward to nowhere-on-earth.
A rumoured place? That takes us to the moon?
Let it be moon. The moon was never more
Than a name without a place to match it . . .
In Deyá there's a moon-blight always

On the watery irises of fancy.
And minds that feed on bodily conceits
Go daft in Deyá, especially Germans . . .
At any rate earth's proved, which saves
The proving of the place it gives into.
And where'd be time for that between
Out of one, into the other, a twinkling
As fast as realizing death—or not?
Therefore, without the learned pause, to find
That Deyá is this open door I say
At least to look in by, if not to enter?

5

Ah, though you can't believe, there's always God.
And that's a story you can go to sleep on
Without waking up next morning
The better or the worse for it.
Indeed, was it not written by yourselves?
A poem's by—who knows? And must be read
In prompt mistrust of the designing sense.
For once you let it have you,
There's no way out unless to leave behind
Your wits in it and wander foolish.
And so you can't believe . . . And yet I speak
With a homely habit of self-pleasing
That tokens reason and a free tongue?
Yes, the possession is my own.
My muse is I . . . What shall we think?
The circumstances are at once
Too natural and too poetical
To determine either doubt or belief . . .
Let's ask Maria, she's cleaning fish
Under the algarrobo with the cats.
Her comb keeps tumbling and her cheek is shy,
But a royal manner clicks in her brain

If the question is important.
And the answer to important questions
Is of course always the same, nor long—
Another question: 'Who asks?'

Let's speak to Juan White-Mule about it
If there's a settlement between
Your certain sanity and mine,
He'll make it, and with no disrespect
To either party, a *paz mallorquina*
Founded on mutual regret
That ever did we meet to differ.
But you'd not like to pledge yourselves
To keep out of my way, as if I were
Not of the same miscellany.
And I could only as usual
Linger apart in tacit presence . . .
Sooner or later you'd strike up talk:
'Peseta's down to-day. What's your story?'
So here's my story, now let me die again
Into the stranger you can't do without,
O tourists of neighbourliness.

PART V

FAILURE OF SEASON

THE SIGNS OF KNOWLEDGE

Not by water, fire or the flesh
Does the world have that end
Which have it must by being, having been,
A world so privileged to begin
And curious long increase of self to have,
And curious long outspinning, spinning out
To end of thread to have—
Not by water, fire or flesh,
Not by drinking back of self,
Not by proud flame of self,
Not by horrid plague to lie down
Sainted, innocented, cruelly gloried—
By words the world has end,
By the words which brought
From first articulation, first stir and stuff,
To the last understanding,
Most and last of world when quiets world
Into a listening and a thinking on
What world it was, into a learning of
What more than most, what later time than last,
Makes full the famished grail
That never rose to brim
With the world's ekèd wine.

By one sign shall you know the end,
The rising to the brim, the passing into plenty,
The full succession, the words enough:
By one sign shall there be a world
More like to wholeworld than your world
More like to mereworld:
By one sign shall you first know All,
See more than world of yours lets see:

By the sign of emptiness,
By an empty grail, an empty world
Of world drained to be world-full.

By one sign! And have you seen?
There is an empty grail,
And nothing, nothing is the world which rose
From bottom of the cup to never-full:
Nothing and never is that world.
And have you seen?
There is an empty grail.
And have you seen?

By two signs shall you know you see.
By two signs shall your much of world
Dissolve and solve into an empty grail.
By two signs shall you know the sign
By which to know an end of world
And fullness forthheld emptily
In full beginning of fullness:
By two signs shall you know you see.

The first sign of the two signs
Shall be unlove of the sun.
The second sign of the two signs
Shall be unlife of the earth.
And the sum of the first and the second sign
Shall be undeath of the moon.
When the moon speaks, when the moon is heard,
When an empty grail glows in the mind
Where once the moon wound faint outside
Like hate of time silenced
To circle-slave in feigned lament of time—
When the first sign and the second sign are one sign

Shall you know the end, the grail, the moon-sense,
Shall the filling up begin,
Shall there be wholeworld pouring brimful
Into an empty grail, an empty world,
An empty whole, a whole emptiness.
The first sign of the two signs
By the knowing of which you shall know
The one sign by the knowing of which
Shall you first know All like grail
Whole at last to brim with All
From whole emptiness of All—
The first sign of the two signs
Shall be unlove of the sun.

Learn then of unlove of the sun,
Lest it be in you and you know it not.
Does your tongue not lazy hang, alick not
With afternoons and aeons like old sores?
It is an old sore, the first sore,
It is all the sores—the sun!
Does your tongue no more sick-pleasure?
Does it stiffen to a taste it tastes not yet?
Does your tongue then point your eyes away
From sights that like old sores lie open
To be pity-pleasures, to be sorrow-scenes
Where beauty festers, frighted to heal?
Does your tongue thirst not to see
The open world, the sunworld sore?
Do your eyes no more with tears burn blind
When thought of otherwhere than sunwhere
Minds your tongue to make command
Of othersights, of mindsights, tonguesights?

From unlove of the sun, by the same glance
Sudden-small to read more true-fine,
Comes unlife of the earth—oh learn,
Lest unlife of the earth be in you
And you know it not, to greet well
What unlove of the sun undarks—
Lest othersights be seen, then lost
In morning-morrow samedark with sunlife.
Learn then of unlife of the earth.

If unlife of the earth be in you,
By a strength to move not shall you know it,
By a weakness against strength strong.
Do your legs awalk leave otherlegs to stand?
Do your hands atouch leave otherhands to fold?
Does your head atwist leave otherhead to straight?
Have you a life, and a life, a quick and a still,
And the quick to lag and to lag,
And the still to tardy allspeed in a
Lasting-over, lasting-other unto-until
Shall come the full of knowsight, knowstep?
Oh, have you vanished from yourself
Nor seek old where-to-be nor new?
Oh, do you break in scatterself and stayself,
In wanderworld and standmind?

Then have you unlife, and learn then.
Undeath of moon has come on you,
The moon-grail clears and wholes,
An emptiness wholeshines at eye-thought.
See whole then: these are the signs.
The first sign and the second sign are the one sign.
The one sign, sign of All, the first truth, first of truth,
Is undeath of the moon by empty grail signed.

The first truth signs an empty grail.
The lesson of the first truth is an empty grail.
The interpretation of the first truth is by the eye.

Rubric for the Eye

See sunwide, worldlong, airhigh;
See waterdeep and earthround.
Then let the eye look whole-impossible,
Look wider, longer, higher, deeper, rounder.
Let the thought sharpen as the eye dulls
Of sharpening on newsights old.
Let the thought see, let the moon be familiar.
Sun of world! Moon of word!
Eye-spilling live of eye! Undeath of mindsight!
Moonclearly, emptily, full grail aspeak!

You have now come with me, I have now come with you, to the season that should be winter, and is not: we have not come back.

We have not come back: we have not come round: we have not moved. I have taken you, you have taken me, to the next and next span, and the last; and it is the last. Stand against me then and stare well through me then: it is a wall not to be scaled and left behind like the old seasons, like the poets who were the seasons.

Stand against me then and stare well through me then: I am no poet as you have span by span leapt the high words into the next depth and season always, the next season always, the last always, and the next always. I am a true wall: you may but stare me through.

It is a false wall, a poet: it is a lying word. It is a wall that halts and does not halt.

This is no wall that halts and does not halt. It is a wall to see into; it is no other season's height. Beyond it lies no depth and height of human travel, no partial courses.

Stand against me then and stare well through me then. Like wall of poet here I rise, but I am no poet as walls have risen between next and next and made false end to leap. A last, true wall am I: you may but stare me through.

And the tale is no more of the going: no more the poet's tale of a going false-like to a seeing. The tale is of a seeing true-like to a knowing: there's but to stare the wall through now, well through.

It is not a wall, it is not a poet: it is not a lying wall, it is not a lying word. It is a written edge of time: step not across, or into my mouth, my eyes, shall you fall. Come close, stare me well through, speak as you see: but, oh, infatuated drove of lives, step not across now. Into my mouth, my eyes, shall you thus fall, and be yourselves no more.

Into my mouth, my eyes, I say, I say. I am no poet like transitory wall to lead you on into such slow terrain of time as measured out your single span to broken turns of season once and again. I lead you not. You have now come with me, I have now come with you, to your last turn and season, which stand you still against me: thus could I come with you, thus only.

I say, I say, I am, it is, such wall, such poet, such not lying, such not leading into. Wait now on the sight, look well through, know by such standing still that next comes none of you.

Comes what? Comes this even I, even this not-I, this not lying season when death holds the year at steady count—this every-year.

Would you not see, not know, not mark the count? What would you then? Why have you come here then? To leap a wall that is no wall, and a true wall? To step across into eyes and mouth not yours? To cry me down like wall or poet as often your way led past down-falling heights that seemed?

I say, I say, I am, it is, such wall, such end of graded travel. And if you will not hark, come tumbling then upon me, into my eyes, my mouth, and be the back ward utterance of yourselves expiring angrily through instant seasons that played you time-false.

My eyes, my mouth, my hovering hands, my intransmutable head: wherein my eyes, my mouth, my hands, my head, my body-self, are not such mortal simulacrum as everlong you builded against very-death, to keep you everlong in boasted deathcourse, neverlong? I say, I say, I am not builded of you so.

This body-self, this wall, this poet-wise address, is that last barrier long shied of in your elliptic changes: out of your leaping, shying, season-quibbling, have I made it, is it made. And if now poet-wise it rings with one-more-time as if, this is the mounted stupor of your ever-long outbiding worn prompt and lyric, worn poet-like—the forbidden one-more-time worn time-like.

Does it seem I ring, I sing, I rhyme, I poet-wit? Shame on me then! Grin me your foulest humour then of poet-piety, your eyes rolled up in white hypocrisy—for I may be one famed sprite more of your versed legend—or turned against me into your historied brain, where the lines read more shrewdly. Shame on me then!

And haste unto us both: my shame is yours. How long I seem to beckon invitation like a wall across which stretches further length of fleshsome traverse: it is your fleshsome shame and my flesh-seeming stand of words. Haste therefore unto us both. I say, I say. Stand hard against me and stare me now well through. This wall reads Stop! ' This poet verses: ' Poet: a lying word! '

Shall the wall then not crumble, as it is to walls given? Have I not said: 'Stare me well through'? It is indeed a wall, crumble it shall. It is a wall of walls, it is a page of very-death, the first. Stare it well through: it is the next and next, the reading gentles near, the name of death passes with the season that it was not.

Death is a very wall: the going over walls, against walls, is a dying and a learning. Death is a knowing-death. Known death is truth sighted at the halt. The name of death passes: the mouth that moves with death forgets the word. The mouth that moves with death stands still the spoken side of truth: it reads and says.

And the first page is the unlettering of death. And haste unto us both, lest the wall seem to crumble not, to lead mock-onward. And the first page reads: 'Haste unto us both!' And the first page reads: 'Slowly, it is the first page only.'

Slowly, it is the page before the first page only, there is no haste. The page before the first page tells of death, haste, slowness: how prophecies fall true now at the turn of page, at time of telling. Truth one by one falls true. And the first page reads, the page which is the page before the first page only: 'This once-upon-a-time when seasons failed and time stared through the wall nor made to leap across, is the hour, season, seasons, year and years, no wall and wall, where when and when the classic lie dissolves and nakedly time salted is with truth's sweet flood nor yet to mix with, be but ensalted tidal-sweet, true-taste, new-taste of true—O sacramental true-and-false and sweet-and-salt by which shall time be old-renewed nor yet another season move.' I say, I say.

BENEDICTORY CLOSE

I have done all, you have done all,
That I, that you, that you, that we,
As I was, you were, we were,
Could have done as doing was.

I have said all, you have said all
That I, that you, that we,
As I was, you were, we were,
Could have said as saying was.

Now comes a blessing on us,
Close all our eyes on us
And let us bless us thankfully
That we have been and are not.

We are not as we were
And as we were was well,
And as we are is well.
It is well now that we are not.

The mystery wherein we
Accustomed grew as to the dark
Has now been seen enough—
I have seen, you have seen.

I have seen and I am off:
I hurry to the cause of it.
You have seen and wait slowly
The forgotten cause of it.

It seems not now distressful
Or to have been then delighted in.
It was a mystery endured
Until a fuller sense befell.

Let us now close our eyes all
And anxiously be blessed in this:
That while I hurry off I bring
The fuller sense back, mystery's cause even.

And while I hurry off you wait,
And while I hurry off I bring,
And while I bring you unforget
The cause which mystery became.

The fuller sense and cause became
That old and older mystery
As you more unremembered
That oldest wisdom you never knew.

And now we have done all, said all,
Within the mystery, you and I,
To make it no blind sudden sight
When open crash the clouds of time.

We have now seen, already seen,
These folded clouds deep through
To blindness, to our evilness
That so have we been wrapped.

We have all sinned, been wrapped apart.
I have gone your way of doing, saying,
You have gone your way of doing, saying,
We have all sinned, pretended.

You have pretended to be seeing.
I have pretended that you saw.
So came we by such eyes—
And within mystery to have language.

The cause was that a way lacked.
It seemed a wayless world like no world.
You made a way and a world
Which no way was, nor any world.

You made that which could not be made.
A way is not to be made, nor a world.
You made no way and no world.
You made a mystery because you made.

You would see, and made a mystery to see.
The cause of the mystery was that you saw.
The cause of the mystery was that you would see.
The cause of the mystery was that you did not see.

There was no sight to see.
That which is to be seen is no sight.
You made it a sight to see.
It is no sight, and this was the cause.

Now, having seen, let our eyes close
And a blind blessing pass among us—
A quick slow blessing to have seen
And said and done no worse or better.

And slowly wait—slowly it came about
A way and a world to be made,
And to seem the way and the world
Which must be if aught is.

Slowly be true as slowly you were false.
By falseness you were,
By your falseness I was false: I was.
Slowly be no more, nor I.

And quickly I: I must be off and back
To come not back but bring back
The mystery's cause and fullness—
The sense comes back, not I.

To you who are not I who am not
Bring that which is if aught is,
That which is if naught else is,
That which is.

My loves, it happens sweet.
It is an oldest wisdom.
Remember what you never knew
And be like stir of knowledge trembling.

Quick and slow within the blindness,
Within the pity we have loosened
After so long upon ourselves
You upon you, I upon us all.

Close all our eyes on us.
A wayless world like no world
Seals the perjurious lids
In pity of them, their eyes.

And what eyes then will open,
And how bright then the way and world
That failed when dull eyes pressed
So bright a sight to see?

It is not so, it is not as it was,
To talk so, see so, study so
A mystery and make so
A sight to see, to dwell in.

We are not as we were.
The action has wearied.
The words will connive no more.
The appearance hangs strange.

We have been in hell.
A blessing on us—we have been in hell.
We have made hell.
A blessing on us—we have proved hell.

There is only hell to prove.
Which logic is a poor art now,
Like to be apt in magic
Where magic is plain guile.

You have no need to prove now,
Nor I to do and say along.
We have finished with the magic.
We have returned to the oldest wonder.

We are now the oldest wonder.
You made yourselves to know.
You now know, you are now unmade.
We are again the oldest wonder.

The oldest wisdom is now known.
To itself is it known.
To itself is it the oldest wonder.
To us is it known.

And we are not, least am I.
First I was a woman, and I feigned.
Then I was yourselves, and I fooled.
Then I was a spirit, and I subtilized.

Now I am not, utterly I am not.
Utterly is that which is.
Utterly I bring that which is.
Least am I, quickest not to be am I.

And slowest you to be not you.
My loves, be slow: wait.
Do not yet go, the end
Is not as you thought—solitary.

The end does not disperse.
It gathers up, it contains.
You shall be destroyed and contained.
You shall be wholly joined.

We shall be wholly joined.
We were then but a patched crowd.
We stood outside us then
Like friendship in vague streets.

And I stood with you,
Against that, soon or sooner,
A blessing and a parting must
Send home to no home.

Against this homelessness
I stood with you, and did, and said.
Here wholly shall we love, meet
And be not, and I least.

A blessing on us all, on our last folly,
That we part and give blessing.
Yet a folly not to be spared:
There is still a greater one.

Were you now to turn ghostly wits
And to say 'Being not, we are not'—
Were you to be found far, as lost,
When the full way and world came finding—

Then must I like myself go calling
Name by name the peevish silence—
This were a greater folly
Than now to bless all.

For in no wise shall it be
As it is, as it has been.
A blessing on us all,
That we shall in no wise be as we were.

I would in no wise again so call.
I shall in no wise again so call.
You shall in no wise again so perplex,
And I with you, in mystery apart.

The cause of the mystery
Was the full sense thereof:
You wished to see fully.
A world is not to be held in an eye.

A world is an eye.
An eye is not to be held in an eye.
A way is an only way.
It is not to be tracked through itself.

Nevertheless it was so,
So indeed you seemed to devise.
So you pretended, and I with you:
We made to be what could not be.

We made an example of ourselves,
You made you to move apart.
I made me a like thing to you.
Thus was it an example, extremely.

For less than you, even, could I so devise.
Where you may once go free
I may not any time.
Where you are many, I am less than one.

I am here fastened, and myself the fastening,
Like no tree in its tenacity.
Like no rock in its stillness:
I am here fastened by that I am not.

It is not I who moved apart.
All but I moved apart.
You moved apart, and I with you,
But I was a dead thing from the first.

As you were live things,
So I was a dead thing.
Such was my likeness to you.
It is like to a live thing to be dead.

For the live thing grows dead.
And the dead thing is not.
Such was your likeness to me.
Such is the joining.

And a blessing on us all,
That we may be joined.
A pity on us all lest it seem not so
By the end of a false friendship.

Therefore close all our eyes on us.
And in such slow voiding do you wait.
For into such slow voiding shall I bring
Quickly the indivisible.

APOCRYPHAL NUMBERS

1
The way of the air is by clouds to speak
And by clouds to be silent.
The way of the air is treachery and repentance.
The air is the freedom to hope.
You breathe your hopes,
And are glad, and live.
And there are clouds.
There are clouds which betray your hopes.
To whom? To your Conscience, which is not you.
And you are ashamed, and the clouds tear.
By the conscienceless air you live,
But by Conscience, your mouth's tight lid,
You die, you are what you are only.
The clouds are you, Conscience is not you.
Yet you make the clouds to tear and repent
For Conscience's sake, which is not you.
For first was the air, and last is Conscience.
And that which is last is, and that which was first is not.
First was freedom, and last is a tight lid.
The free word tears, but more silent the closed mouth.
The air opens your mouth, the clouds dissolve it.
Conscience closes the mouth, but gives it back.
What is Conscience? It is Death.
And being dead, are you not Death?
No, being dead you are Death's loved ones only
Speechless with pride to be so silent
Against the clouds which steam in treacherous whispers
Repentantly your mouth round, dissolution's aura
Of tattered hopes, grieving as you dare not.

2

Yet it is not all immaculate death—
Not all a folding to of covers
Punctually, by time's trembling hands.
There is (unreadable) a stained clatter
After that day of instantaneousness
Has spread instantly its lasting night.
There is a motley panic of steps
Along remembered streets which take backwards
Into longer days as into bedrooms
Late with morning sleep, timeless.
It is not all a tidy ending, dawning
Of a picture-page whereon tidily, briefly,
The world is told of by a thinnest light—
The moon-like smile of worn Forgiveness.
Against this weather-peace there cries (unhearable)
A red wind, as the sun once bellowed,
And a black rain beseeches, as earth once
Coaxed with itself to be more bold.
It is not all this guarded day you keep
Whose foreheads cleared this day and found you
Hiding in it from old insanities,
Garrulous headaches, mute bodily debates.
This night which hammers brain-like
At your immune memories now
Lies far and dim, but great it lies
As far and dim, greatly it unrolls
That which has been forgotten greatly.
It is not all this narrow day.
There is that, also, which you have forgotten.
There is a lasting night abroad,
And though you lock it in itself

With lockless rigour, that it may not out
By any mercy-key of yours,
Still is it one with this inexorable page,
Since of you also those heaped chapters
Toward which, as to later days,
Starved, later selves of you go futuring.

3

Nor is it written that you may not grieve.
There is no rule of joy, long may you dwell
Not smiling yet in that last pain,
On that last supper of the heart's palate.
It is not written that you must take joy
In that not thus again shall you sit down
To spread that mingled banquet
Which the deep larder of illusion spilled
Like ancient riches in time grown not astonishing.
Lean to the cloth awhile, and yet awhile,
And even may your eyes caress
Proudly the used abundance.
It is not written in what heart
You may not pass from ancient plenty
Into the straitened nowadays.
To each is given secrecy of heart,
To make himself what heart he please
In stirring up from that fond table
To sit him down at this sharp meal.
It shall not here be asked of him
'What thinks your heart?'
Long may you sorely to yourself protest
This single bread and truth,
This disenchanted understanding.
It is not counted what loud passions
Your heart in ancient private keeps alive.
To each is given what defeat he will.

ADDENDUM

THE FIRST LEAF
AND
THE SECOND LEAF

THE FIRST LEAF

I say myself.
The beginning was that no saying was.
There was no beginning.
There is an end and there was no beginning.
There is a saying and there was no saying.
In the beginning God did not create.
There was no creation.
There was no God.
There was that I did not say.
I did not say because I could not say.
I could not say because I was not.
I was not because I am.
I am because I say.
I say myself.
Myself is all that was not said,
That never could be said
Until I said 'I say'.
I say.
I say myself.
How am I now who was not, yet never was not?
What is now?
When is now?
What am I?
Who am I?
Where is now?
Where am I?
I am, I never have not been,
Perfect agreement thing with thing.
Never was there not
Perfect agreement thing with thing.
I say perfect agreement thing with thing.
I say myself.

Never was I not.
Never has there been not now.
I am now because never was I not.
I am now because time is not.
I was not because God was.
Time is God.
God was time.
Time is thing on thing.
God was perfect disagreement thing with thing.
Never were there not things.
Never was there not
Perfect agreement thing with thing.
Never was there God.
Time is a noisy silence.
God did not say.
God did not create.
Never was there creation.
Never were there not things.
Never was there not
Perfect agreement thing with thing.
Perfect agreement thing with thing is to say.
Never till now has it been said.
I say.
I say myself.
What is now?
Now is myself.
Now is when I say.
What am I?
I am what I say.
Who am I?
I am I who say.
Where is now?
Now is where I am.
Where am I?

I am in what I say.
What do I say?
I say myself.
What is myself?
Myself was not God.
Myself is not time,
I say God was not and time is not.
Now is perfect agreement thing with thing,
Which never has been not.
Now is not thing on thing,
Which never is.
Now is all things one thing.
Time is not.
What is a thing?
It is that which, being not myself,
Is as myself in being not myself.
What is one thing?
It is all things myself
And each as myself
And none myself.
For I alone say.
I alone say myself.
I say myself only.
There is myself to say only.
There is one thing to say only.
There is one thing only.
Myself alone is the one thing only.
I am not I.
I am the one thing only
Which each thing is
When each as all is
In being each only.
I am not I.
I am not I,

Though none other but myself am I.
I am the I which is not any one.
I am no one.
I am I.
I am not I.
To be myself has taken time, all time—
Has taken thing on thing, all things—
Has taken God, thing with thing not one thing.
To be myself has taken life, thing and thing—
Has taken death, thing and thing and nothing.
To be myself has taken to be not myself.
It was not myself, it is myself.
Now is I.
I am not I.
I am now.
Before now was a world.
Now is I.
A world is a before.
A world has no beginning.
A before has no beginning.
A before always was.
A now always is.
Never was now.
Always is now.
Never was I.
Always am I.
I am whatever now is always.
I am not I.
I am not a world,
I am a woman.
I am not the sun which multiplied,
I am the moon which singled.
I am not the moon but a singling.
I am I.

I am my name.
My name is not my name.
It is the name of what I say.
My name is what is said.
I alone say.
I alone am not I.
I am my name.
My name is not my name.
My name is the name.
The name is the one word only.
The one word only is the one thing only.
The one thing only is the word which says.
The word which says is no word.
The one word only is no word.
The one word only is agreement
Word with word perfectly.

THE SECOND LEAF

Suspicion like the earth is hard
And like the earth opposes
Dense fact to the doubtable:
Which therefore like the air surrenders
Semblance to the bolder sights.
I have surrendered place
To many solid miles of brain-rote,
To the just so many matters and no more
That reason, grudging prodigal,
Allows numerous, consecutive.
Even in my own mind I have stood last,
An airy exile, nothing, nowhere,
My eyes obeying laws of circumspection
By which myself shone fanciful
In lurid never:
Because that had been so, I not.
But as time learns a boredom,
Loathes the determinate succession,
Irks with uncalendared event
And brings surprise to be,
The natural conscience snapped in me—
And lo! I was, I am.
Elastic logic thinning
Grows delicate to marvels.
Fine argument unclews at finest
The ravelled accurate maze of caution.
The sudden of the slow is bred,
The curious of the common.
Into the sceptic fog that mists
Infraction from the chronic rule

Stumbles intelligence arage
To find the unthought wanton thought
And, self-confounding, think it.
My life, with other lives a world,
With other ways of being a coiled nature,
Springs separate: I have estate,
Of being caught in that pressed confluence
And proven self-substantial,
Counterself of the familiar soul,
In fellowed course entwined
Acquaintance marks out unacquaintance.
Usage has bound of mystery.
The continents of vision view
A further which grows spatial
From lying next; in dark increase
Of the gregarious light with which
Compacting sense embraces straggling all.
Thus is reality divided
Against itself; into domestic axiom
And recondite surmise;
And joins when near to uttermost,
When plain to covert leaps,
In one extreme of here-to-here.
I have a local likeliness,
Haunting the various neighbour-hearth;
But where the shadow is and chill
And unwalled distance night-deep,
I also am, or was, and not, intolerably.
Must be union of body, and wraith.
Wonted and wondrous must touch.
At first there's daze, habit's reluctance.
Then quivers new that which loured archaic
Which has the secret age enough
To open frank from bloom potential

Like the last flower of nervous chance,
And the first of far intention.
But is this I interior,
The smothered whole that lurked identical
Till obvious fragment sought
Its late entire and matching?
Or the outer stranger, proofless,
Come from stealth into defiance
And with a heart incongruent—
Suspicion's devilish shadow
Which the lies are made of,
For truth-proud reason to declare untrue?
This is I, I: the I-thing.
It is the self-postponed exactitude,
An after-happening to happen come:
As closing calm is worn to actuality
By all the sooner winds, and these
Its wild own are, in heirship silent.
A soft word-fit ear to meet
With a monster-distant noising—
Be it of lapsed vigours fallen
Furious at their meaning's ebb—
In the same room of sound is ominous:
There's word to be, and hearing of it
Louder than these memories
Which once, being life, itself, prevented.
So have I beat against my final ear
Past whims and whirrings, stubborn echoes
Whose lost persuasion I made my own,
Whose dinning death. So have I lived,
Approaching rhythms of old circumstance
To the perilous margin, promptest moment.
And struck the string which breaks at sounding,
Taken the tremorless note to mouth,

And spoken sound's inversion
Like a statue moved with stillness.
This is that straitened all-risk:
An I which mine is for the courage—
No other to be, if not danger's self.
Nor did I become other, others,
In braving all-risk with hushed step,
Mind rattling veteran armouries.
I did thus creep upon myself
A player of two parts, as woman turns
Between the lover and beloved,
So it be well— she is herself and not,
Herself and anxious love.
So it be well, the clasping, death of fear.
When passion smooths into a face
And madness tames from scream to voice,
And dumb impossibility
Mantles aflush with language:
So is it well, the danger.
We have rejected time,
Ravished the furtive future
From our coward lag-clock;
And nothing's left to count but now,
And now again, and then and then
That cannot but be same,
That may not flutter strewn,
Spreading its instant unity
As it were lazy flock of bird-speed.
If this be I.
If words from earthy durance freed
To earthy right of self
Cannot belie their wisdoming,
The doubt-schooled care that bent back sense
From skyish startle, faith's delirium.

If I my words am,
If the footed head which frowns them
And the handed heart which smiles them
Are this very table, chair,
This paper, pencil, taut community
Wherein enigma's orb is word-
constrained.
Does myself upon the page meet,
Does the thronging firm a name
To nod my own— witnessing
I write or am this— it is written?
What thinks the world?
Has here the time-eclipsed occasion
Grown language-present?
Or does not the world demand,
And what think I?
The world in me which fleet to disavow
Yields mind to longer thought?
And these the words ensuing.

APPENDICES

'With the Face': forebeing grows of age

WITH THE FACE[1]

With the face goes a mirror
As with the mind a world.
Likeness tells the doubting eye
That strangeness is not strange.
At an early hour and knowledge
Identity not yet familiar
Looks back upon itself from later,
And seems itself.

Today seems now.
With reality-to-be goes time.
With the mind goes a world.
With the heart goes a weather.
With the face goes a mirror
As with the body a fear.
Young self goes staring to the wall
Where dumb futurity speaks calm.
And between then and then
Forebeing grows of age.

The mirror mixes with the eye.
Soon will it be the very eye
Soon will the eye that was
The very mirror be.
Death, the final image, will shine
Transparently not otherwise
Than as the dark sun described
With such faint brightnesses.

1

Amid the strenuous struggles of the longer poems of *Poet: A Lying Word* are studded several serene and perfectly-realized shorter poems, of which 'With the Face' is a beautiful example; 'Earth' and 'The Flowering Urn' are others. This essay begins with an account of how the poem works technically and then attempts to elucidate its meaning, showing how the poem relates to words and themes from her wider work.

The first point to make is how the poem begins, as do so many of her poems, with statements of elementary limpidity and strength. In her preface to *Collected Poems* the author wrote:

> Because I am fully aware of the background of miseducation
> from which most readers come to poems, I begin every poem
> on the most elementary plane of understanding and proceed
> to the plane of poetic discovery (or uncovering) by steps which
> deflect the reader from false associations, false reasons for reading.[2]

The poem provides a good example of that, and of what Clark describes as 'that cumulative power of *statement*' in her poems.[3] It could be said, as with other of her poems, to begin with an almost glaring simplicity but to end with an intricate and darkly mysterious precision. This progress is reflected in the rhythm of the poem: each stanza begins with a series of brilliant short statements, but each ends in a more intricate, simultaneously complex and concise, and — in the final stanza — clinching resolution.

The second point to note is the use of parallelism and repetition with variation and development (and intensification). Parallelism, 'careful alternation of images' and 'the recurrence of ideas in varying alternations', were commended by Riding and Graves in *A Survey of Modernist Poetry* as means to a 'regularity of design more fundamental than mere verse regularity'. There the techniques were applied particularly to the 'problem' of longer poems, but a review of Riding's shorter poems show that the same techniques are regularly deployed in them too.[4] The poems mentioned above, 'Earth' and 'The Flowering Urn', are further examples.

In 'With the Face' the opening four lines are paralleled by the first six lines of the second stanza and by the first four lines of the third. The opening pairings of internal and external (face/mirror, mind/world) are expanded and developed in the second stanza (reality-to-be/time, mind/world, heart/weather, face/mirror, body/fear) and then they are condensed and unified in the first four lines of the third:

> The mirror mixes with the eye
> Soon will it be the very eye.
> Soon will the eye that was
> The very mirror be.

There is a similar parallelism and intensification and development, or uncovering, in the last four lines of each stanza. The language of the first stanza concerning time, and the relationship between past, future and now (the 'early hour' looking 'back upon itself from later') is paralleled in the second stanza ('Young self' and 'dumb futurity'). The final four lines of the poem parallel and draw together strands of thought and imagery from the whole of the rest of the poem: 'Death, the final image', for example, combining ideas relating to the face/mirror and to the end of, or compacting of, time.

Complementing those larger parallelisms, there is a fluidity and suppleness of movement between the first and second parts of each stanza. For example in the first stanza 'That strangeness is not strange' is reflected two lines later by 'Identity not yet familiar'; then 'And seems itself' is echoed by by 'Today *seems* now' (italics added). This in turn leads into the elaborated sets of inner/outer pairs in which the 'With the mind goes a world' precedes 'With the mind goes a mirror' in order to lead into a new association 'As with the body a fear', which prepares us for 'Young self goes staring to the wall.'

2

The poem begins with statements of utmost simplicity: 'With the face goes a mirror|As with the mind a world.' Without a mirror the eye could not see itself, or the face; without a world the mind could not understand itself. But for all the apparent simplicity of most of its component parts it is not possible fully to understand this poem in isolation from others in the collection. After the clarity of the first two lines we come upon: 'Likeness tells the doubting eye|That strangeness is not strange.' 'Strangeness' is referred to and explored in several of the poems of *Poet: A Lying Word.* 'The Way It Is' ends with the lines

A most improbable one it takes
To tell what is so,
And the strangest creature of men
To be his natural self.[5]

This can be related to Riding's consistent view that 'the poet, if a true poet, is one by nature and not by effort', but that the modern poet is beset by the demands of criticism and the professionalization of poetry.[6] It is therefore not easy to be natural but if one focuses upon oneself, and upon the mirror, eventually the apparent strangeness (of oneself and of the world) is not strange. The poem 'Short of Strange' has the lines:

Think you this strange?
But think you not woman strange,
And strange as death indeed,
Stranger than God-you?

The idea of strangeness there can also be related to this poem's line 'Young self goes staring to the wall' (where 'the wall' contains the idea of both the mirror and the world, and 'staring' contains the ideas of fear and steadfastness in facing apparent strangeness) and to the lines from 'There Are as Many Questions as Answers':

And what is to be born?
It is to choose the enemy self
To learn impossibility from.

An analysis of the fourth line of the second stanza, which seems to stand on its own, 'With the heart goes a weather.' helps us to understand the author's thought in relation to 'strangeness'. In 'A Preface to a Second Reading' of *The Telling* the author wrote:

We look for surprise and variety in our daily encounter with the nature of our being as if it were weather-like: our curiosity towards our human-being imitates the curiosity of body we have towards the weather. But the nature of our being is not to be known as we know the weather, which is by our sense of the momentary. Weather is all change, while our being, in its human nature is all constancy. Humanness, though belonging to many, does not vary. We are inconstant in it, and so can be curious towards it as if it were itself inconstant. But it is to be known only by the sense of the constant.[7]

'Identity', to move on to the next lines of the poem, is another word, or theme, referred to and explored by other poems in *Poet: A Lying Word*, beginning with the final lines of the opening poem 'As to a Frontispiece:

That is, as you may guess,
I have a work but, I regret,
No preliminary portrait.
And if you can forgo one,
We might between us illustrate
This posthumous identity.

In 'After Smiling' we have the lines:

Now is my smile pursed smooth
Into a stillest anger on
All flesh convivial
To my convivial flesh
Like scattered selves of me
Insisting right of scatteredness
And homed identity both—
As if by smiling promised.

While this approach, by the use, in effect, of concordance, is helpful in understanding the work of this most careful and con-sistent poet, the disadvantage is that it can create a whirling 'scatteredness', a centrifugal effect on our reading, it takes us outwards, and this effect has to be complemented by a renewal of centripetal attention on the poem, or the 'homed identity', itself.

The author's thought in respect of time has also to be understood in order to appreciate the poem. What does she mean by these lines?

> At an early hour and knowledge
> Identity not yet familiar
> Looks back upon itself from later,
> And seems itself.

> Today seems now.
> With reality-to-be goes time. [...]
> Young self goes staring to the wall
> Where dumb futurity speaks calm.
> And between then and then
> Forebeing grows of age.

The first four of these lines may seem baffling unless one recognizes that implicit in them is the vision that was later to find fuller expression in the author's 'personal evangel', *The Telling*. Certain passages there give an indication of the thought behind her earlier, poetic work.

> We [we humans, unlike other creatures] do not stop at our
> bodies, but outstrip them. We are more than our bodies, and
> can remember what was before them. They [the 'creatures
> of limited being-range'] can have no memory of a Before
> [...] Not from them have we evolved, but from spirit's blind
> effort, called 'nature', to form perfect beings ... in whom
> Being shall be recomposed, from its universal sunderedness.

> They are marvels, wondrous errors, creatures of accidental
> excellences, that astound; but we are creatures suffused with
> nature's whole intention.[...] My wish is, in asserting our
> relationship to nature to be direct, and a primary one for it
> and us, to defy the legend of the closer identity with nature
> of creatures of other life-walks. It is a foolish diffidence to
> think we are more strangers to nature than they. [...] Yes, I
> think we remember our creation!— have the memory of it
> in us, to know. Through the memory of it we apprehend
> that there was a Before-time of being from which being
> passed into what would be us. [...] Souls there were not
> until there were bodies in which, each, diversity's extremes
> were brought into a union; ... another and another and
> another, to that rounding-in and exhaustion of diversity
> which is human. Thus from physicality emerge persons
> — ourselves.[8]

How breathtakingly risky this seems, this is! However, the
account is not totally unprecedented. It has kinship to Keats'
description of the World as a Vale of Soul-Making, in particular
his statement 'There may be intelligences or sparks of the
divinity in millions—but they are not Souls until they acquire
identities, till each one is personally itself.'[10] In her 'Addendum' to
The Telling Mrs Jackson refers approvingly to these statements by
Keats, and also at greater length to Coleridge:

> The theme of what I say is expressed in "I have made visits
> to the human actualness of my being". Coleridge has written:
> ... the greater part of mankind cannot be prevailed upon to
> visit themselves sometimes; but according to the saying of
> Solomon, *The eyes of the fool are upon the ends of the earth.*

She also refers to Coleridge speaking of 'an antecedent unity'
comparing that with her own references to 'the all-antecedent
reality' and 'an all-familiar One-image—our before'.[11] In the
poem in view her later prose is anticipated, in part at least, by her
lines 'With reality-to-be goes time' and then:

Young self goes staring to the wall
Where dumb futurity speaks calm.
And between then and then
Forebeing grows of age.

Surprisingly my (1971) Oxford English Dictionary did not list
'forebeing' which would have made it appear to be a neologism.
It is surprising because the word appears in the title of 'From the
Night of Forebeing', a well-anthologised long poem by Francis
Thompson, a poet Riding praised highly in her early poetic man-
ifesto 'A Prophecy or a Plea' (1925) as one who 'made his soul the
agent of perfection in an imperfect life'.[10] There are lines in 'From
the Night of Forebeing' that are reminiscent of the beginning of
Riding's poem, for example:

My little-worlded self! The shadows pass
In this thy sister world, as in a glass,
Of all processions that revolve in thee [...] (108-110)[11]

The effect of the line 'Forebeing grows of age' is to tie the end
to the beginning, as she vividly describes herself doing in one of
her fragments:

'I shall mend it,' I say,
Whenever something breaks,
'By tying the beginning to the end.' ('Echo 11')[12]

The last two lines of the second stanza mirror and develop the
meaning of the first two lines.

Riding's use of 'age' in opposition to 'time' again repays atten-
tion. In her poem 'In Nineteen Twenty-Seven' she wrote:

Then, where was I, of this time and my own A
double ripeness and perplexity?
Fresh year of time, desire
Late year of my age, renunciation [...]

'My age' is what I have made 'my own', or what I have made of
myself by seeing clearly, and refusing to succumb to the temptations
of 'experience', or of the Zeitgeist. It reminds one of the gravestones

which dignify the deceased as having died in the particular year of their age.

3

The face needs a mirror, as the mind needs a world, in order to know itself. Jacobs' brief but incisive account of the final stanza of 'With the Face' makes a good starting point for a re-reading of the poem:

> The poem is the means of fusing inner and outer, what is with what is seen, self and image, and earlier in the poem, mind and world. There is no difference, only sameness, between one's self and what one perceives, or to put it another way, the universe, in its seeming largeness, is present in the human self, in its seeming smallness, and both are combined in a poem.[13]

The poem deals not just with space but, as we have seen, with time. She was fully aware of Einstein's theory of relativity and met the challenge of the new scientific thinking in the person of herself, and in her poems (and prose), just as Coleridge had met the challenge of philosophical and scientific materialism (in prose argument and poetic practice) at the beginning of the nineteenth century.

The final four lines of the poem remain mysterious:

> Death, the final image, will shine
> Transparently not otherwise Than
> as the dark sun described With
> such faint brightnesses.[14]

Why is the sun 'dark'? And to what does the 'such' in the final line refer? In *Poet: A Lying Word* 'With the Face' is placed in Part II which opens with 'All Things', a poem that introduces and describes the place of the sun in Riding's cosmology. That poem ends:

> An observation of my—
> What shall I call such patience
> To look back on nature,
> Having already looked enough

> To know the sun it is which was,
> And the sun again which was not,
> By nights removed from self,
> By nights and days, by souls
> Like little suns away toward
> Dreams of pride that could not be—
> What shall I call such patience—
> An observation of my agedness—
> Death's long precision while
> All things undo themselves
> From sunhood, living glory
> That never, never was—
> Because the sun.

Note here the use of 'agedness', and how it relates to the use of 'age' in the passages quoted in section 2 above.

The first two of 'The Signs of Knowledge' (in the poem of that name) are 'unlove of the sun' and 'unlife of the earth':

> And the sum of the first and the second sign
> Shall be undeath of the moon.
> When the moon speaks, when the moon is heard,
> When an empty grail glows in the mind
> Where once the moon wound faint outside [...]
>
> Then have you unlife, and learn then.
> Undeath of moon has come on you,
> The moon-grail clears and wholes,
> An emptiness wholeshines at eye-thought.
> See whole then: these are the signs.

And in the final passage of that poem, the italicised *Rubric for the Eye* she opposed *'Sun of world! Moon of word!'* Later, in *The First Leaf* she wrote:

> I am not a world
> I am a woman.
> I am not the sun which multiplied,

I am the moon which singled.
I am not the moon but a singling.
I am I.

Putting these clues together we can see that in the process of the poem in view the mind (or the 'moon of word') has brought the 'sun of world' to an end in 'death's long precision'. The poet has 'undone' herself 'from sunhood', from its spurious fecundity, in order to create a final image described with faint but precise brightnesses (as perhaps, although she does not say so directly in 'With the Face', of the moon).

One way of reading the last four lines is as an actual total-eclipse image, where the solar corona provides the 'faint brightnesses', 'described' being used in the sense of 'outlined'.[15] It suddenly occurs to one that it is the moon (of word) that stands before the sun (of world) in such an eclipse, 'intervening' literally rather as the author herself commented:

> My moon may look like the tired old poetical symbol, and I like an old tired poetic romanticist, but I truly meant that the moon's being what it is where it is intervenes in our outer circumstances as a negator of the sun's fostering excessiveness in our regard, both lush and destructive—as a tempering counter-agency, relatively little but near.[16]

4

In this book of her poetry 'The Signs of Knowledge' and *The First Leaf* serve as the most explicit and 'unpoetic' sets of statements which provide the background which allows the condensed poetic beauty of 'With the Face', 'Earth' and 'The Flowering Urn', and later poems such as 'Doom in Bloom' and 'Nothing So Far' to function serenely and concisely — poetically even. 'The Signs of Knowledge' focuses upon her cosmogony of earth, moon and sun, and illuminates the relation of word and world. *The First Leaf* patiently sets out the poet's definitions of creation, time, God, of 'things' and brings it all together in such equivocal and unequivocal statements as:

Now is I.
I am not I.
I am now.
Now is I.
A world is a before.
A world has no beginning.
A before has no beginning.
A before always was.
A now always is.
Never was now.
Always is now.
Never was I.
Always am I.
I am whatever now is always.
I am not I.
I am not a world,
I am a woman. [etc]

'What courage!' as the poet and critic G.S. Fraser once said of Riding. To expose one's hand so completely and baldly, to invite scorn. And yet, as she said, concluding the commentary (given at the end of the previous section) on her account of the sun and the moon:

> However foolishly mystical this may seem, nothing so far learned by scientists or [...] experienced by astronauts disproves this.[17]

Endnotes

1 In later editions of this poem there is one tiny variant, a comma replacing the full-stop after 'calm' in line 16.

2 *Collected Poems* (London: Cassell, 1938) xvii.

3 In his review of the 1980 edition of *Collected Poems:* Alan J. Clark, 'Where Poetry Ends', *PN Review*, 1981, No 22, 26-28; quotation from p27.

4 'The Problem of Form and Subject Matter' in *A Survey of Modernist Poetry*.

The quotations here are taken from the Carcanet edition, *A Survey of Modernist Poetry* and *A Pamphlet Against Anthologies* edited by Charles Mundye and Patrick McGuinness (Manchester: Carcanet, 2002), 23. Riding's use of parallelism, and her responses to the poetry of the Bible merits further study. Parallelism was recognized as the key poetic method of biblical verse as long ago as 1753, by Bishop Lowth, but has only been systematically explored in the last fifty years, notably by Robert Alter, *The Art of Biblical Poetry* (New York: Basic Books, 1985, revised 2011).

5 In *Collected Poems* the last two lines were changed: 'And the strangest creature of all|To be natural.'

6 This quotation is from *Contemporaries and Snobs* (London: Cape, 1928), 124. In her 1938 'Preface to the Reader' Riding wrote of the dishonesty of attributing the compulsion of poetry to forces outside oneself, such as divinities and muses, religion, politics and mythology. 'When one feels compelled to do something because one wants very much to do it from one's own point of view, then it is dishonest to put the onus of compulsion on some outside force —one only does this by way of excusing one's failures.' *Collected Poems* (London: Cassell, 1938), xxii.

7 Laura (Riding) Jackson, *The Telling* (London: Athlone, 1972), 62-63.

8 *Ibid.* Quotations from pp 27-28 and p30, parts of passages 27 and 28. Readers of Teilhard de Chardin will feel that there is some affinity between what Mrs Jackson says here and some of his work. She clarifies the differences between them in a long note, pp155-159.

9 *The Letters of John Keats,* selected by Frederick Page (Oxford: OUP, 1954), 266.

10 The references to Keats and Coleridge come in Mrs Jackson's fascinating 'Addendum' to *The Telling* (1972), 177-185; quotation from p184.

11 'A Prophecy or a Plea', first published in *The Reviewer*, 5 (2), April 1925, 1-7; republished as Appendix C to *First Awakenings*, (Manchester: Carcanet, 1992), 274-280. Thompson gives as an epigraph to his poem a quotation from Sir Thomas Browne: 'In the chaos of preordination, and night of our forebeings.'

12 'Forebeing' also appears in one of Riding's last poems, 'In the Beginning':
That was not the genesis:
This is the genesis.
That was the impregnation

Of the Mother by her children-to-be
Who in the fluster of forebeing
Cried out in voiceless voice:
'We are the Father!'
Then voice of voice: 'I am the Father's Son!'

14 Mark Jacobs' 'Preface' to *Collected Poems; The Poems of Laura Riding* (New York: Persea Books, 2001), xx-xxi.

15 I was reminded of this 'transparently' when reading a passage in Philip Rowland's essay '"Celebration of Failure": The Influence of Laura Riding on John Ashbery': 'Turned in upon itself, challenging its very right to exist, the poem, in her hands, becomes act rather than object, transparence rather than thing.'

16 I owe the idea of a total eclipse of the sun to a suggestion from Alan Clark, responding to an previous version of this essay. There is humour in the idea of the 'female' moon 'of word' blotting out all but 'faint brightnesses' of the 'male' sun 'of world'.

16 'Excerpts From A Recording (1972), Explaining The Poems', in the centennial edition of *Collected Poems; The Poems of Laura Riding* (New York: Persea Books, 2001), 496.

17 Ibid.

SELECT BIBLIOGRAPHY

Joyce Piell Wexler, *Laura Riding: A Bibliography* (New York and London: Garland Publishing, 1981) provides a more detailed bibliography for this period.

A. Selected editions of the poems

Though Gently (Majorca: Seizin Press, 1930). Edition limited to 200 copies.Reprinted as a special insert in *Delmar*, Number 8, Winter, 2002, together with eleven essay responses including 'Some Bibliographical Notes' by Alan J. Clark.
Twenty Poems Less (Paris: Hours Press, 1930). Edition limited to 200 copies.
Laura and Francisca (Majorca: Seizin Press, 1931). Edition limited to 200 copies.
Poet: A Lying Word (London: Arthur Barker, 1933).
Collected Poems (London: Cassell, 1938), with a preface 'To the Reader'.
The Poems of Laura Riding (Manchester: Carcanet, 1980), a reissue of the 1938 *Collected Poems* with a new 'Author's Introduction'.
The Poems of Laura Riding: A newly revised edition of the 1938/1980 collection with a substantial centennial preface by Mark Jacobs (New York: Persea Books, 2001). Appendix V gives the fascinating 'Excerpts from a Recording (1972) Explaining the Poems' by Laura (Riding) Jackson.

B. Contemporary criticism by the author

'A Prophecy or a Plea', *The Reviewer*, 5(2), April 1925, 1-7 (reprinted in Appendix C of *First Awakenings*, 1992, 275-280).
A Survey of Modernist Poetry by Laura Riding and Robert Graves (London: Heinemann, 1927).

A Pamphlet Against Anthologies, by Laura Riding and Robert Graves (London: Garden City, 1928). Both reprinted in *A Survey of Modernist Poetry* and *A Pamphlet Against Anthologies* by Laura Riding and Robert Graves edited by Charles Mundye and Patrick McGuiness (Manchester: Carcanet, 2002).

Anarchism Is Not Enough (London: Cape, 1928); reprinted and edited by Lisa Samuels (University of California Press: 2001).

Contemporaries and Snobs (London: Cape, 1928); reprinted and edited by Laura Heffernan and Jane Malcolm (University of Alabama Press, 2014).

D. Significant criticism

Joyce Piell Wexler, *Laura Riding's Pursuit of Truth*, (Ohio University Press, 1979), especially Chapter VII, pp68-78.

Elizabeth Friedmann, *A Mannered Grace,* the authorized biography of Laura (Riding) Jackson, (New York: Persea Books, 2005) contains biographical context to, and commentary on, some of the poems.

Michael Kirkham, 'Robert Graves's Debt to Laura Riding', *Focus on Robert Graves*, 3 (December 1973), 33-44.

Jack Blackmore, *The Unthronged Oracle* (Cirencester: Mereo 2016), Chapter 1, and Chapters 10-14.

Mark Jacobs, *The Primary Vision* (unpublished).

Acknowledgements

My especial thanks are due to the editor of Nottingham Trent Editions' Laura (Riding) Jackson series, Mark Jacobs, who was reduced to the rôle of (not entirely uncomplaining) galley-slave in the the production of the text of this book. That repetitious and arduous labour was in addition to his advice, and questioning, and encouragement at every stage.

Alan Clark, with his unmatched memory for the particulars of Laura (Riding) Jackson's work, found errors that several readings had missed, and made crucial suggestions on a number of points, particularly in relation to the essay on 'With the Face'.

I have valued Joyce Wexler's generous encouragement in response to work in progress.